PE...

THE T...

'Hilarious. The laughs and life lessons are ten-a-penny' *STYLIST*

'Hilarious and highly relatable. The perfect gift for anyone who loves a good laugh' *WOMAN'S OWN*

'Warm and sprinkled with celebrity stardust. Urges us to embrace our most embarrassing moments, instead of agonizing over our humiliation' *SUNDAY EXPRESS*

'These warts-and-all stories are as funny as you'd expect, as warm and supportive as you'd hope, and liberally sprinkled with celebrity stardust' *DAILY RECORD*

'Amusing behind-the-curtain anecdotes' *TELEGRAPH*

'Will make you laugh, and will then make you walk into any room and be your absolute self. Dawn French: Legend, Icon, Actual Twat' DAWN O'PORTER

'Dawn French is a national treasure. Loyal, self-deprecating and garrulous, her stories make for entertaining reading' *MAIL ON SUNDAY*

'This woman is a warm hug in human form, spreading joy in abundance. She is dazzling' LORRAINE KELLY

ABOUT THE AUTHOR

Dawn French has been making people laugh for 30 years. As a writer, comedian and actor, she has appeared in some of this country's most long-running and celebrated shows, including *French and Saunders*, *The Vicar of Dibley*, *Jam and Jerusalem*, and more recently, *Roger and Val Have Just Got In*. Her first three novels, *A Tiny Bit Marvellous*, *Oh Dear Silvia* and *According to YES*, are all *Sunday Times* bestsellers.

DAWN FRENCH

The Twat Files

Illustrations by Jessika Green

PENGUIN BOOKS

UK | USA | Canada | Ireland | Australia
India | New Zealand | South Africa

Penguin Books is part of the Penguin Random House group of companies
whose addresses can be found at global.penguinrandomhouse.com

Penguin
Random House
UK

First published in Great Britain by
Penguin Michael Joseph 2023
Published in Penguin Books 2024
005

Set in Bauer Grotesk Pro

Printed and bound in Great Britain by Clays Ltd, Elcograf S.p.A.

The authorized representative in the EEA is Penguin Random House Ireland,
Morrison Chambers, 32 Nassau Street, Dublin D02 YH68

A CIP catalogue record for this book is
available from the British Library

ISBN: 978–1–405–94727–5

www.greenpenguin.co.uk

FOR KRIS HALLENGA
A CONFIRMED AND MASSIVE TWAT

Ad gloriam macularum

Wanker. Git. Prick. Prat. Dick. Eejit. Plonker. Pillock. Nincompoop. Bellend. Dolt. Chump. Nitwit. Fuckwit. Lunatic. Dork. Numskull. Idiot.

All lovely . . . but . . . nah . . .

I prefer Twat.

It's neat and it's accurate somehow.

It was acceptable to my mum and it has a bit of bite, but doesn't hurt really. There's something satisfying about how wide your mouth stretches to say it, and the plosive 't' that bookends the word is a total joy.

Feels tight and pointy. Pointed. Suits me.

I've used it so very often, and I've been called it even more. I don't take offence. I know it's an admonishment, but somehow it's also inherently affectionate, so it's OK.

I came to realize that the twattish moments in my life are at the forefront of my memory when I was attempting to write an autobiography. This was annoying. I wanted to present myself as an interesting, sophisticated, semi-heroic, multi-layered person, y'know – not a cacking twat . . .

It seems that being an actual twat is much more authentic, the real me, almost my forte, if I may say so. The more I thought about it, the more I understood that the moments where I've made mistakes – misunderstood stuff and messed up – were key. That's where all my tinging clear learning happened, and it has always been where I laugh the most. Who doesn't want that?!

I opened the floodgates and started to jot down notes about the many twatty incidents I'd been party to over the years. It was a tsunami. Time and time again, I've been a massive eejit. Sorry to boast, but I really am a champion twat. I'm accomplished.

Once I'd finished my initial wave of cringe, I decided the only way to shake off any feeling of shame or embarrassment was to collate some of the stories and devise a show to tell them out loud. I did that. I loved it. I experienced the BEST EVER connection to the audience because, of course, being a twat is universal and my twattishness is no different to yours. Except, perhaps, that mine has been horrifyingly public on occasion. There wasn't room in the show for all the stories I wanted to tell – so – here they are, for your delectation.

I can't emphasize enough the freshness of the air I breathe since I decided a few years back that being perfect was impossible. I've always known it deep down, but like so many of us, I wasted too much time pointlessly trying to capture it. Why?

Nowadays, not only am I certain it's impossible, but I wholeheartedly know, with my whole whole actual heart, that it's not even desirable. In fact, I'd like to abolish it, and start an anti-perfection league where we can celebrate our shortcomings with glee. That way we can hop over the hurdles of nasty that are the self-harm of imperfection and enjoy the release of running on the flat (floppy bosoms allowing), where all the sweetness and fun is, right to the finishing line. I promise you, there is abundant joy to be found in our flaws.

A treasure chest of glittering defects awaits, if we would only share, and I'm urging you to start now and allow your own mistakes to amuse you. It's a powerful ol' tool, believe me. A valuable resource.

My hope would be that reading these stories might fire up yer engines to remind you of just what a massive twat you also are, that we might celebrate and revel in this most delightful of traits, together.

I'm thinking I may have to organize some badges so that we can proudly recognize each other when we're out and about. Perhaps we can give one another awful high fives that sort of awkwardly miss...? That would be perfectly twatty.

Anyhoo – I hope you enjoy.

NASCENT TWATNESS

When I was very young, I was massively influenced by television. And comics.

Two TV shows I really loved were American. *The Partridge Family* (my first virtual encounter with long-term crush David Cassidy) and *Bewitched*. Much as I loved the comedy, the music and the stories, it was the leading women who grabbed my attention, namely Laurie Partridge and Samantha Stephens. Not only did they individually have an extraordinary set of particular skills, but they were both stunningly beautiful. I wanted to be like them, so I tried to work out how to borrow some of their allure. What was it about them?

Well, Laurie had the cutest little button nose and tons of freckles, and Samantha had the cutest little button nose that wiggled independently of all the other muscles in her face. Impressive. So, that must be the winning formula – a cute twitchy nose and freckles.

So, that's what I did. At around age thirteen, I deployed these techniques in the desperate hope of securing some kind of attention from boys. I painted fake freckles on my cheeks and across the bridge of my nose with dots of brown eyeshadow, and I perfected an alarmingly quivery scrunch with my nose that I felt sure was irresistibly 'cute'. It wasn't. I looked like a demented rabbit. My friends can testify to this.

Add to that sorry image a rictus grin. I like to blame my darlin'
dead grandmother for my lifelong propensity to show EVERY

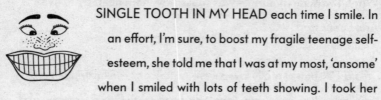 SINGLE TOOTH IN MY HEAD each time I smile. In
an effort, I'm sure, to boost my fragile teenage self-
esteem, she told me that I was at my most, 'ansome'
when I smiled with lots of teeth showing. I took her
very literally on this and followed her instructions to a 'T'. I wanted
my entire denticulation to be on show. Every last chopper, all gum,
tongue and lip should be proudly displayed in a leering grimace
worthy of the most rabid of wolves. I can confirm that the heady
mixture of demented rabbit and confused wolf was not, repeat
NOT, successful in luring boys on to my pubescent rocks. For some
inexplicable reason, it emphatically didn't work. It was an epic fail. In
fact, boys actually fled. My smile revulsed them. They ran screaming.

OK, so that mistake was a long time ago. I was young and naïve.
You would think I'd learn. Indeed, I no longer crinkle my nose in a
rectum-clenching awful attempt at cheesy cuteness. I no longer
paint freckles on to my face.

However . . . for some reason I cannot logically understand, I have
persisted with the rictus grimace. I can't seem to stop myself, even if I
actively pre-warn myself NOT to do it. Put me anywhere near a camera
and bingo – there she blows – the fang-meister general – the queen of
snarl – the wholly desperate-to-please TWAT! Thanks, Grandma.

Childhood twatting is surely very easily excused in general. I think most of us have claimed to:

- be related to a Royal

- have 'toxic' blood

- have been raised by wild creatures in a forest

- know how to speak 'cat'

- have the genitals of a Martian

- have a witch and a wizard for parents

- be Elvis's illegitimate daughter

- be a person with an ageing condition that means you may look nine years old, but you are in fact eighty-two

- have had a brain transplant with a genius

- have been personally asked by the Beatles to be their backing singer

- been the baby Stevie Wonder is singing about on 'Isn't She Lovely'

- have secret gills that mean swimming underwater for miles is no prob

- have a personal actual angel (invisible) Jesus has appointed to look after you

- have met Aslan and Mr Tumnus in person

- be allowed to drive your parents' car regularly

- have a Russian pen pal who writes to you in actual Russian and yet, miraculously, you can read it fluently

- have a pet swan

- have a mother with three breasts

- be able to control your robot brother with a hand-held device

- have found a secret tunnel to the Tower of London in your garden near Lincoln

Well . . . haven't we?!

Oh – just me then. WOW.

I wasn't entirely unfamiliar with the odd fib, y'know, to liven things up a bit. Surely that's normal? I remember when my own daughter submitted a song she'd written for a music exam piece at school, a song she titled 'Looking from a Window Above'. The song was very, very good. Mainly because it was 'Only You', written by Vince Clarke and sung by my close chum Alison Moyet. Good try, junior twat.

We used to get quite a lot of things wrong in my family. Not big, important stuff, we didn't murder anyone . . . well, not on purpose. We were quite contained, kept ourselves to ourselves, so I think we might have been somewhat out of step with certain trends or fashions. My parents bought a teasmade (google it, kids – a machine that made your tea for you in accordance with an alarm, right next to your bed!) just as everyone else was discovering how singularly useless they were. That sort of mistake.

I sometimes felt that we were slightly 'outside' somehow. Maybe this is not unusual. I didn't know where we belonged – not geographically, not economically, not in terms of class, not socially. It might be to do with being in an Air Force family. The itinerant nature of our life during my childhood meant we couldn't settle easily. Not in any category. We sorta ploughed our own furrow, which meant that we floundered sometimes, trying to work out how to fit in. One such example was when my lovely dad got it a bit wrong when he responded to my teenage longing for a pony. I constantly mithered him about it. I'd had some lessons and fallen in love with the whole notion of owning a horse. It's the first real love affair that some teenagers have and, frankly, it's a more rewarding experience than trying to secure the affections of another human. Horses are IT. Big, powerful, hairy, huge eyes, long lashes, soft-as-velvet noses, give fantastic heavy-breathing-type snuggles into your neck, never betray you, don't get drunk, never get bored when you talk. There are so many reasons to have a horse instead of a boyfriend. Especially if you haven't actually got a boyfriend, and nobody actually seems that interested in you.

One day, my dad struck a strange deal with a bloke who owned a garage near where we lived in Cornwall. A man who owed the garage owner a debt offloaded two horses he didn't really want on to the forecourt of the garage and my dad brought these horses home for me. A chubby chestnut mare and her wall-eyed foal. I named her Shula and him Marty, after Marty Feldman, because his eyes were weird. Anyone who really knew anything about horses (we didn't) would know that this was categorically NOT the right fit for me. Shula was not young. We had no idea how old, but she was certainly tired.

She wanted to be left alone to munch grass, thank you. Marty mainly wanted to bite my tits, which he did often. Along with Shula came an old saddle and a bridle, so we assumed she'd been ridden somewhere along the way. There was no girth with the saddle. That's the bit that connects it from side to side, going under and around the horse's belly, like a thick belt. Instead, at first, we tried an actual belt, but that was rubbish and didn't attach properly, so Dad had the genius (not) idea of making a girth from an old tractor tyre. There were plenty scattered about on the farm we were renting at the time, and he thought it was a shame to waste them ...

He set about it and it took ages, but eventually he had something approximating a large belt, to which he attached buckles to either end. I wished SO HARD we could've just bought a girth like everyone else, but it felt ungrateful to say it after all the effort. He also took some time to soften and clean the leather of the tack. He used warm, soapy water and then rubbed oil into the brittle, cracked, thirsty leather. He probably should have used specific saddle oil, but it's our family, so he used vegetable oil, which was sort of OK, but didn't smell great on sunny days.

During the spring, when Dad was doing all this work to fix the tack, something alarming happened.

One of the main reasons to have a horse at all if you are a teenage girl is to groom it. This involves hours of brushing with many different implements called weird names like Curry Comb or Dandy Brush or Rub Rag. Soft brushes, hard brushes, finishing brushes, you name it, I spent my pocket money on it. I had no real idea what to do, but it all meant spending hours upon hours in a stable stroking and brushing my beloved equine amour. Manes and tails are key. The combing, the plaiting, the styling – it all MATTERS VERY MUCH. It is how you love your pony.

Imagine the horror, then, to discover that my horse had a previously hidden disease called 'Sweet Itch', which is something to do with the grass in springtime and which means that the ENTIRE mane and tail FALL OUT each year, leaving your bald horse with a scabby reptilian dinosaur neck and tail for months before it gradually restores itself. Your horse is a stegosaurus. Crossed with a rhino. Hardly a horse at all. I wept about this abhorrence for weeks, it was so shocking. Of course, I didn't want Shula to feel any responsibility or shame for her wretched condition, so I never cried a tear in her presence. I was brave. I still cuddled her, but it was sort of revolting to snuggle up to her rough, scabious neck. She was, without doubt, mangy.

The Royal Cornwall Show is a big deal. It happens in Wadebridge, right next to the farm we were living on, pretty much every June. It's a celebration of all things Cornish and rural and joyful and we loved it. There are horse events at the heart of it. Show jumping and displays and judging and things and things and horsey things . . . including a gymkhana. I didn't really know what this word meant until I went to the Cornwall Show. It's basically competitive games on horseback. The gymkhana was open to anyone to participate, so long as they had a pony. I'd watched it often and dreamt of taking part, if only . . . if only . . . I had a pony.

And now, I did.

The gymkhanas were full of smart pony-club girls in just the right gear riding just the right ponies. There was a dress code I didn't know. There was a huge, wide horsey world of knowledge I simply didn't have. I didn't know that jodhpurs had to be a certain colour for certain events. I didn't know that neckties had to be appropriate, or jackets, or covers on helmets, or anything, frankly. I just loved my scabby pony. So, I took her there to take part.

The first race was already going to be a problem. It required us to canter to the end of the arena, grab a plastic cup from a pole and canter back. First back wins. Shula was ancient, she didn't move fast by choice; this was going to take plenty of encouragement in the form of yelling and giddy-upping from me.

That's the me in my dad's tweedy gardening jacket and my wellington boots.

That's the Shula in the ill-fitting saddle, which smelt like a breakfast fry-up, and with a tractor tyre awkwardly gripping her sizeable undercarriage. The disdain from the other contestants on the starting line was palpable. They clearly found the chubby girl on the chubby, glabrous horse hilarious. We were patently no threat to their shiny, athletic perfectness, both riders and horses.

Really? We'd show them.

I'd seen horsey films. In practically all of them, the underdog (underhorse?) always comes steaming through on the unexpected inside to steal the victory.

I could taste it, that victory.

I'll show them.

The whistle blew and off we went. Quite slowly at first. Shula was reluctant. Eventually, after loud proclamations including the cry 'You bugger!' quite a lot, she sped up into a gentle trot. All the others reached their cups quickly and were on the return journey, whizzing past us the other way, by the time we reached ours. My fantasy wasn't manifesting ...

That was irritating, but what happened next was twat-level, lemon-stingingly humiliating to a degree I'd not experienced before. As we rounded the pole and I retrieved the cup, Shula seemed to finally get the message that speed was of the essence and so she broke into a surprising canter for what, I suspect, was the first time in her life. Probably unused to the sudden jerkiness of the speedy movements, the saddle started to slide. Clearly, the homemade girth wasn't quite fit for purpose. As the saddle travelled sideways, so did I. The shift of weight shocked Shula, so she bolted even faster. The girth came looser. The saddle travelled further south. The pony was basically hoola-hooping the saddle around her body, with me attached. There was, for a brief, surreal and painful few seconds, the fact that I was riding my scabby pony entirely upside down with her hooves bashing into my head on every stride. Of course, I soon fell right off and was dragged for a few horrifying moments before Shula stopped still to basically munch some grass and process the unusual fact that her saddle was hanging down between her legs.

I stood up, dripping with disgrace, took a deep breath and walked to my pony, straightened the saddle back up and left the arena, being sure not to hear any remarks or to look anyone in the eye. We walked out of the Royal Cornwall Show, crossed the road and kept walking the next mile or so home.

I might as well have had 'TWAT' seared on to my forehead with a branding iron, so red-hot with embarrassment was I.

It wasn't my fault.

It wasn't my dad's fault.

But it was utterly absurd, and the only way I could think of to recover from the lingering nip of that drenching ignominy was to retell it. As I have done here. For your amusement, and for mine. That way I can harness anything self-conscious or uncomfortable about it. It remains silly that way, and not shaming.

Yep, I rode a horse upside down like a proper twat.

TEENAGEHOOD

There were many ongoing examples of sweet twattery throughout my teenage years, mainly when I felt vulnerable or embarrassed. Dating boys was a giant arena of squirm. In the comics I read, girls behaved differently with boys. They put on quite the display – often feigning a kind of shy stupidity to convince boys they needed protection. Or something. This was a brand of girliness I just didn't know how to do. I knew it worked on boys though – I'd seen my own brother fall hook, line and sinker for big, gooey eyes and batty eyelashes. We came to know this behaviour as DWB – meaning Different with Boys. I was hopelessly awful at it. The pretending to be a totally other sort of person didn't sit comfortably with me. I gave it my very best effort though. On top of the freckles, the nose scrunch, etc., I decided to deploy a 'cute' reaction I'd seen in a comic once. A boy was kissing a girl and when they finished, she licked her lips and said, 'Mmm, sugar,' while she blushed and fluttered at him. There's always that awkward moment at the end of a kiss, isn't there? It's already been a bit strange, what with all the tongue intrusion and slobbery-smacking noises. Really, what I wanted to say was, 'Mmm, sloppy,' but I knew that wasn't flirty enough. I needed to find something I could repeatedly use and adapt, so I decided to use various different flavours instead, depending on the boy. It did get out of hand, the more embarrassed I was:

'Mmm, strawberry.'

'Mmm, lemon.'

'Mmm, lollipops.'

'Mmm, marshmallows.'

As time went on, I started to get more literal ...

'Mmm, lager.'

'Mmm, chips.'

'Mmm ... fags ... ugh.'

It didn't work at all. Probably because it was entirely fake and utterly cringeworthy. I ended up actually scoring the kiss ...

'Umm, four out of ten ...'

'Umm, never again, sorry ...'

'Umm, little to no interest in repeating that ...'

'Umm, bye ...'

This was prime twat behaviour and it has since ceased, you'll be relieved to know.

I have boasted unashamedly in the past about folk I've kissed. I absolutely LOVE kissing; it might be my favourite hobby. After castrating toads or smoking crack, that is, of course . . . Joke. Don't cancel me.

But seriously, I've been lucky enough to kiss some seriously dishy folk . . . usually for comedy purposes. However, no kisses EVER will surpass the raw carnality of the teenage kisses that took place up against the wall in the car park opposite Burgh Island in Devon.

My girlfriends and I would pile into my little Morris Minor (it was round and black, so it was nicknamed 'The Bomb') on a Saturday night, and head from Plymouth to Burgh Island, about an hour's journey. I would park up in the corner of the dark car park and we would wait . . .

and wait . . .

and wait . . .

Eventually, the sea tractor would hove into sight, bringing the revellers back over the flooded causeway from the notoriously dodgy disco in the hotel on the island. The passengers would disembark and go on their way home, presumably. Except for a particular group of boys, who would head towards their motorbikes in the corner of the car park where I had strategically parked.

We would get out of the car, saunter over casually and stand by the wall next to the bikes. The boys would be ignoring us, smoking cigs and laughing. We would be ignoring them, not smoking cigs, but definitely laughing, if only to prove that we were having just as much fun as them and couldn't care less whether they noticed us or not. This was high-level active disdain.

As if on a complicit silent secret cue, the boys dashed out their smokes, walked over to us and, without a single word being uttered, we would lock lips and snog furiously against that naughty wall for a full-on fifteen minutes. No words were ever spoken. All you could hear was the slurping of the kissing, the thrilling squeak of their leather jackets against us and the squawking of irate seagulls spying on the writhing, furtive teens below.

No actual sex happened, but plenty of sex happened, and it was MAGNIFICENT. They would unlatch from us on cue, put on their helmets and walk to their motorbikes without a backward glance, clamber on, fire up the engines and zoom off into the night, leaving us re-applying our lip gel and quivering at the electrifying sensation those throbbing engines left us with. We'd get back into The Bomb and burst into hysterical screams about how mind-blowingly exhilarating it all was. Heady stuff. I don't think I will be kissed quite like that ever again.

I guess it was flirting really. Without the flirting.

We behaved in a similar way when we regularly met a group of boys from Plymouth College each Friday after school in a café called GoodBodies. They sat at one table, we sat at another, PURPOSELY ignoring them. We actually used to physically turn our backs on them and mutter insulting things under our breath about them. We'd do this for an hour or so, then leave. There was virtually NO CONTACT whatsoever and yet . . . it was scintillating. This hour of snubbing behaviour would nourish us for a whole week until we could repeat it again. We all understood the insane rules of behaviour. No one crossed the line into actual interaction. This strange, disconnected flirting was somehow enough. The promise of it was sufficient. More than sufficient.

It was phenomenal.

We were cluster-twatting.

Flirting has never ever been a skill I've mastered. I'm in awe when I witness people doing it with ease on dating shows, etc. For me, it's the ultimate cringe, and a rich seam for my twatty leanings to surface.

When I was a smelly student at drama school, on a teacher-training course, I developed a crush on a beautiful boy on the acting course. It was standard practice for the actors to look down their noses at us since they believed that we were obviously people who had failed to get on the acting course. We weren't. We were people who wanted to be teachers. Anyhoo, my penchant for this particular actor was consuming me. I would constantly fantasize about him, which dripped into actually dreaming about him, so he was all over and in and next to my thoughts day and night. I tried to place myself where he might notice me. I started to learn his timetable, so I knew when he might be posily slouching about, like actors do, in the common parts of the college. Don't get me wrong, I'm not a crazy. I didn't want to wear his skin . . .

Well, not much.

I simply wanted the opportunity to have a conversation with him.

Call me cocky, but I genuinely believed that if he could only get to know me, he would surely fall completely in love with me. I've never doubted my worth (thanks, Dad), but I was having to face the fact that he simply wasn't making himself even slightly available to fall under my seductive spell. In fact, he didn't seem to have noticed me at all. How very odd. And unfortunate. For him.

I needed to rectify this immediately, so I made a spontaneous decision to move in on him and use my sparklin' repartee to talk him into submission, surrender and, eventually, bed. Natch.

I took a deep breath. I would need air for this mission. I approached him. His back was to me in the foyer where he was perusing the timetables on a big noticeboard. That was to my advantage. I could arrive at his side by stealth, as he might well have fled if he'd seen me approaching.

'Hi.'

He jumped back and turned to face me. I could see a little curl of revulsion in the corner of his eminently kissable mouth. No matter. For my ploy to work, I needed to plough on undaunted. Pretty soon, he would get the joke, laugh uncontrollably at my naughty, impish allure and spontaneously fall pretty heavily in love . . .

'So, hey, we've been here at college together for nearly three years now and you've been too intimidated by what a Bobby Dazzler I am to approach me. Well, that stops right now, Mister, because I give you full permission to get to know me. Inside and out. Here we go, hold on to your hat (he wasn't wearing one). So . . . my full name is Dawn Roma French, the middle name is inherited from my mother and I believe is Romany in origin, exotic, I agree. I was born in Holyhead in 1957 and, lucky for my mum, I was a baby at the time . . . '

I wait for a laugh. None comes. This technique is floundering. I press on . . .

'I was a chunky child, a real rusk-taker . . .'

Nothing? These were my best gags. Sadly. I decided to drop the obvious jokes, just go for over-info . . .

'I have a brother who is two years older than me. I have a mole in my left armpit. I have all my own teeth. I am of good stock and good reputation – as yet unsullied by rumour or gossip, although there's plenty of me willing to do something gossip-worthy, if you get m'drift, young gentleman, m'lad . . .'

Nothing. No response. I am a hopelessly beached whale. He looks as if he's smelled something rancid. He has. My desperation. I persist . . .

'No doubt you will be wanting to know about all my inoculations, swimming certificates, bank statements, brownie badges and smear tests? Yer luck's in, matey, I got 'em all in this here pocket . . .'

At this point, he slid along the wall and bolted for freedom.

Epic fail.

Shame, really. I had TONS more of this hilarious, coruscating patter about my childhood and, indeed, my entire life to impress him with. His loss . . .

. . . his one and only chance to build a fabulous relationship with an ocean-going twat.

———————— ✳ ————————

One very clear 'wake-up-you-twat' moment I had concerning kissing happened on the set of *The Vicar of Dibley* when we were doing a Comic Relief special that featured Johnny Depp. The real Johnny Depp. Johnny Actual Depp.

I know.

The scene required Alice (Emma Chambers) and me to knock on the door of his Winnebago and invite him to a party at the vicarage with Sarah Ferguson, the Duchess of York.

I know.

The producer walked us over to Johnny to say hello. He's a fan of Brit comedy and a total all-round mensch for saying yes to this little sketch. As we approached, Emma was squealing with anticipation and clutching my hand in excitement. It was infectious. Not giving me an actual infection . . . I mean her delight was catching and I started to breathe differently as we approached him. He turned and I genuinely went from short breaths to zero breaths. He is properly beautiful. That kind of handsome that seems impossible. He is delicate-looking, nearly female in his softness. I was afraid to breathe lest I broke his exquisite face with my hefty British air. Somehow, I managed to speak without any puff escaping from me whatsoever.

'Hello, I'm Shlawn,' I croaked. I don't even know my name. I'm tipped up by the sheer shine of this ruddy gorgeous fellow.

'Hi, Johnny,' he says, using normal air for breathing, and knowing his name perfectly well. Unfazed. He is cool and collected.

I am not.

I am ruffled and unhinged.

He leans towards me and for a wondrous microsecond, I believe he wants to cement our instantaneous attraction with a full-on lip kiss. Why wouldn't he, for dogs' sake?

This is the moment, surely, from which there will be no returning. We will chuckle and remember it fondly when we recount it to our many grandchildren in our seventies. The moment we both knew that this giant love was gonna be forever, was gonna be the kinda love they would wish for themselves in the future. Gan-gan and Pop-pop – who fell in love on the spot when they met and kissed . . . all those millions of years ago. Yeah . . .

Anyway . . . very quickly it became obvious he was aiming for my cheek in an affectionate, utterly non-sexual way. He did go a bit European and go for BOTH cheeks, so I took the opportunity to aim my lips both ways, just like that sideways emoji with the heart kiss, in a pathetic attempt to have some sort of lip contact, however slight. As he drew back from me I saw myself reflected in his eyes – a maternal figure he completely respected, a homely, matronly type, a perfect vicar. This was raw platonic. There was nil desire. At all.

He viewed me as sexless. A neutered and spayed being, someone who, if he thought about me for long enough, would help him to instantly lose any erection, should he need to.

It was sobering, for sure, to feel so massively temperate and unsexy. I clearly wasn't in the ring when it came to contenders for Johnny's amorous attentions. I wasn't even in the building. Or the country. Or on the planet.

I felt crushed by this realization.

I'd never thought of myself as disregardable. So, I walked away . . . and had a major word with myself.

What the helling cock was I even thinking?

It had nothing whatsoever to do with my value to him. Or even my value to myself. It was a plain and simple moment where two people met who don't have to fancy each other. He didn't have to. He had a girlfriend. He was being decent. It just wasn't there. I was the one who was giddy, who was stupidly influenced by all the hype about an insanely famous, beautiful man who must then, surely it follows, be a lothario. In that case, his kindly approach would be a sure rejection?

It's total bollox. Here was a perfectly lovely bloke just turning up to do his job. He had excellent manners, was nothing but polite and professional and FRIENDLY. Just a bloke. Not a reputation.

If I was going to take all that as some kind of personal rejection, and be complicit in this idiocy, well then, I'd better check my GIANT ego and have a little chat with the twat in the mirror. Shut it, Frenchie (slaps own face), and . . . onwards, with slightly dented wing mirrors.

PANTO

I have a friend called Gareth who is a really good musical theatre actor. When I was about twenty-five, Fatty Saunders and I went to the Kenneth More Theatre in Ilford to watch him starring as Prince Charming in the panto *Cinderella*. He is extremely handsome and, like all heroes in pantos, part of his role was to sing lots of crowbarred-in current pop songs to his leading lady, however inappropriate. Jennifer and I were lapping it up while he was giving his best 'Eye of the Tiger' and 'Let's Get Physical'.

We were at the back of the stalls, in the middle of the row, munching sweets and laughing a lot. I love panto. I love the sheer Christmassy joy of it, the traditions and the silly stuff.

There came the moment when Buttons did a bit of audience interaction. Lovely. This was what we loved, we expected, we came for. When Buttons was on stage, we knew there was going to be games and fun and prizes.

It's important at this point that you should know I have never really won a prize in my life. Not bingo, not tombola, not lucky ducky fishing at the fairground. I don't tell you this to elicit sympathy, I tell you because it might help to understand what happened next. I'm pleading mitigating circumstances in advance, is what I'm doing.

So, we were sitting there, and Buttons announced that there was going to be a big prize for whoever had THE MAGIC NUMBER on the back of their programme. I started casually fishing about in my voluminous bag at my feet to find my programme. Meanwhile, Buttons was holding the prize aloft as if it were Simba, showing it to us, the whole kingdom. It was one of those trolls, remember the ones we used to stick on top of our pencils? With the brightly coloured sticky-up hair and staring eyes? Naked and rubbery and stumpy-fingered and orange? It was one of those . . . but HUGE, the size of a toddler. I adored those trolls as a little girl and the sight of the massive one did something to my stomach. It kick-started a sudden and overwhelming covetous need. I wanted it. I wanted it bad. More than any twenty-five-year-old rightly should.

So, I was looking at the troll, desiring it badly, but thinking I wouldn't get it because I never win anything, and I was scrabbling to look at the back of my programme – just in bloody case.

Finally, I found the programme and turned it over to find the MAGIC NUMBER on the back, and yep, just my luck, my unluck, the number on my programme was 13. Of course it was. Clearly, I wasn't destined to own that gorgeous troll, ever. Typical. Shame.

Buttons called for hush and reached into a glittery bucket to choose a random number. Everyone in the auditorium went quiet. He chose a number and announced it with a flourish:

'The winning number is ... number thirteen!'

Oh. My. Actual. God.

It was me!

My skull exploded with joy. This was the stuff of my best dreams; I could hardly believe it. I jumped out of my seat immediately, shouting, 'Buttons! Over here! I've got thirteen! It's me! It's me!' I could feel Jennifer tugging at my sleeve to sit back down. She was embarrassed. Or jealous. Either way, I ignored her and started to shove my way past everyone in my row to get to the central aisle.

'S'cuse me, s'cuse me, can you just – s'cuse me, now, please!'

Why didn't they tuck up their knees and let me out quicker? Grrr.

Excuse me, I'm the winner.

Excuse me, I'm the actual champion.

I got to the aisle at last and started a little victory trot down the length of the stalls towards the stage. There was a sort of low roar that went up. Yes, they were willing me on – everybody loves a winner, don't they? And I was that winner and, like the noble victor I was, I broke into a little gallop and I shook my mane as I charged ahead. God, it felt wonderful to be THIS great. I was winning at life, baby.

I was nearly at the stage now.

I was within touching distance of the wondrous prize.

It was so very nearly mine . . .

The audience was really loud, and I was grinning with all my teeth like the rabid wolf I was. The winning wolf, that is.

I arrived at the stage and I reached up for my reward. Give it to me. Now.

Buttons leaned down and whispered something to me. I couldn't hear him because of all the laughing. LAUGHING? Why were they all laughing so much? Too much.

I leaned in and finally I heard what he was saying:

'It's a joke, love. EVERYONE has number thirteen . . .'

Oh.

No.

PLEASE.

GOD.

NO.

Everyone had number 13. Of course, they did. It was obvious.

Everyone in that theatre got that joke.

Everyone but me.

There were rows and rows of very special 'care in the community' folk – they got the joke.

There were elderlies in the advanced stages of dementia – they got the joke.

There were three-year-old toddlers – they got the joke.

I, however, did not.

The gallop I proudly took on the journey to the stage took ten seconds.

The walk of shame back to my seat – dear Lord, the shame – that took five years.

What a prize twat.

Jennifer had her head in her hands and mumbled, 'Just sit down,' to me when I eventually reached my seat.

'I just really wanted it . . .' I replied, pathetically.

'I know,' she said. 'We all know . . .'

GLASSES

There are too many incidents of twat to mention when it comes to my experience of motherhood, but one story sticks in my craw. I don't think I even have a craw, but this sticks there, so that's proof of how strong the memory is.

When my daughter Billie was about eleven, she showed me a picture in a magazine. It was the wonderful Kate Moss advertising some very cool spectacle frames. They were black with a sort of filigree detail. I can't remember who the designer was, but the frames would certainly have been expensive.

Billie was asking if she could have these. I sat her down and went into some detail about the fact that they were prescription glasses and that she didn't need them, that they weren't just a fashion accessory.

She insisted that she wanted them.

I gently re-iterated why she couldn't have them.

She pulled a grumpy face and stomped off.

Bratty behaviour, I thought.

So – a week or so later, she came home from school and informed me that she'd made an appointment at Specsavers in Reading for the following week. The girl is nothing if not tenacious. I had to admire her determination. She wanted them beauticious frames!

'OK,' I said, 'if you are going to pursue this madness, I will take you to my optician in London. Then perhaps you will believe me that you don't need glasses and, trust me, when you understand that – I will NOT be putting plain glass in those damn expensive frames so that you can look cool.'

I booked a date for an eye test with my friend Steenie, the owner of The Eye Company in Soho and tip-top spectacle historian. I knew he wouldn't take any nonsense from her. He put his very best optician on the job, and I accompanied Billie into the small, dark back room for her test. Now we have you, madam, I thought. I had quietly warned the optician that her sole purpose was to secure the fancy frames and he reassured me that there was no way she could fool the test, he would know.

The lights dimmed; the test began. He projected the ever-decreasing letters on to the wall and I sat while she attempted to convince him that she couldn't even see the big letters. Honestly, I thought, she could've been a better actor! It was foolish of her to try her scam right at the outset. Not particularly subtle. I started giggling quietly to myself. This kid was going to be so busted.

The test finished, and he put the lights back on. He sent her out of the room to have some water and wait outside. Here we go. He's going to give me the hilarious truth.

He certainly did that.

'Yep,' he said, 'she is SEVERELY myopic. No doubt whatsoever. She can only see objects right in front of her nose. If it's more than an arm's distance, it's a total blur. Her world is completely reduced. I can't believe she hasn't been run over by a car. All of her other senses will be working overtime to compensate. She certainly won't be able to see a blackboard in a classroom; she probably can't really see the teacher. I'm surprised she can find the classroom. Or the school. This kid needs serious glasses. Immediately.'

I was stunned. Although I didn't doubt for a second that she desperately wanted those particular frames, what she was really asking for was sight! She had incrementally gotten used to not being able to see much at all and was living in a close-up world of confusion. She didn't want that any more. I realized also in that very sobering moment, that I had TOTALLY assumed she wouldn't need glasses yet because I didn't until I was forty or so. It's in the genes.

Then I remembered.

We don't have the same genes. She is adopted.

I honestly NEVER THINK ABOUT THAT!

AAAAGH!

The optician gave her some temporary contact lenses that were closest to her actual prescription and would last her until her new glasses were ready.

I watched her look around in awe as she saw our amazing world in focus for the first time. It was fantastic to see, but I felt like a total twat for not noticing before.

Needless to say, her first glasses were the beautiful and very expensive Kate Moss frames.

COMIC STRIP MOMENTS

I suppose that when you work with the same group of people for lots of years, there are bound to be plenty of twatty moments, and my years of working with the Comic Strip were a rich seam.

The very, very, very first bit of filming I ever did was for a little arthouse film we made called, of course, *The Comic Strip*. I don't think a single soul saw it. It was one of those punky indie films. Julien Temple directed it and he was hotter than a hot thing at the time, so we were all very excited to work with him.

The film was set in the Comic Strip club, which was in a tiny theatre called the Boulevarde inside one of Paul Raymond's strip clubs in Walker's Court in Soho. It featured all the original Comic Strippers, so that's Ade Edmondson, Rik Mayall, Nigel Planer, Pete Richardson, Alexei Sayle, Arnold Brown, Jennifer and myself. It centred around the acts we did on stage, but there was a hilariously tenuous backstory where Jennifer played a good Christian girl coming to rescue her slutty sister (me) from the horrors of Soho nightlife . . .

I know.

HOW TO BE
A TWAT

So, the time came for my first-ever scene in front of a camera. It was set in one of our actual shabby dressing rooms backstage – a long, narrow room with make-up mirrors down one side and sinks on the other. Jennifer was standing at the far end, and I was to enter the room and have a shouty scene with her. The camera was set up in the doorway looking towards Jennifer; sort of my point of view of her. The director Julien instructed me to stand level with the camera and to deliver my lines to her from there.

This worried me enormously. I thought it meant I wasn't going to be in the scene because I clearly wasn't in the shot.

What nobody had explained to me, of course, was how filming worked. The basic rules of a single camera, e.g. that you film a scene one way, then you place the camera on the opposite side of the room and shoot it all again the other way, and then you eventually edit it all together.

I did NOT know this. For some unfathomable reason, I didn't work it out for myself even though, truly, it's quite obvious. So, I started to panic . . .

Julien placed me level with the camera and shouted 'Action!' and in my misguided desire to be seen, I spontaneously hatched a plan . . . Jennifer spoke the first few lines – tumpty, tumpty, tum – then came my turn. I sprang into action, pushed past the camera and, in a bold display of extreme twattery, I walked to the centre of the room where I turned and, inexplicably, delivered MY lines directly to camera. Lines that were patently meant to be spoken to Jennifer. Tumpty, tumpty, tum. Rather pleased with myself, I finished my line and returned to my assigned position next to the camera.

Jennifer, although somewhat startled, battled on and delivered her next line – tumpty, tumpty, tum. Then it was me and I repeated the whole debacle once more, racing to the middle of the room and turning to address the camera directly with my lines – tumpty, tumpty, tum.

At that point, the director shouted, 'Cut!' very loudly. He approached me.

I smiled, hopefully. He said, 'What exactly are you doing, for God's sake?'

I replied, 'Making a film, I think.'

He then took me aside and explained the basic rules of filming to me and, in my humiliation and as the extent of my obvious twatness dawned on me, I tried to dig my way out of it by saying, 'Ohh, I see, you're filming this THE OLD-FASHIONED WAY! You're taking the TRADITIONAL route. I was doing something a bit more avant-garde, bit more MODERN ... but hey, look, you are the director, fine, so let's do it your way. Of course. No problem. Right. Let's go ...'

And I returned to my position by the camera, chirpy and ready to go.

On the outside, confident and willing, if a tad 'revealed'.

On the inside, shuddering with mortification from top to toe, from bum to breasticles.

I outdid myself there, truly excelling at twat.

And, as is so often the case, everyone there knew it.

———————— ✳ ————————

We went on to make over forty films as the Comic Strip, and I tried my very hardest not to be a total jerk. Sometimes I succeeded. Often, I didn't.

One such moment occurred when we made a film called *Consuela*, a parody of *Rebecca* that Jennifer and I wrote together. We were delighted that revered director Stephen Frears agreed to direct it. We were a bit in awe . . .

Jen played the first Mrs Saunders and I played the Mrs Danvers part, a sinister maid called Consuela. I wore a very sombre black dress with a pristine white collar and an apron. The apron had a pert bow in the back at my waist. Stick with it . . .

Joining our fairly large crew on the set was a brand-new rookie costume assistant trainee called Hannah, and she was charged with the job of making sure the bow was always neat and perky. It's an understatement to say that she took the job VERY seriously. Her eyes were laser-fixed on the bow and at any given opportunity, whether it was appropriate or not, she would be repeatedly jab, jabbing at my back, in her efforts to straighten it.

I tried to be sympathetic.

'Hannah, look – thanks for your diligence with this blummin' bow, you're ever so meticulous with it . . . erm . . . but I'm not quite sure you understand how this filming lark works. Honestly, we ALL make mistakes when we start out, I certainly did, but . . . let me just suggest that you stick by that monitor over there, and you can see that this shot we're doing is just on my face, so we don't see the bow at all, so no need to fiddle with it, if that's OK? Thanks anyway though . . .'

But no, she stopped twiddling with it for five minutes max. Then . . . jab, jab, jab – she was at it again!

'Hannah, sorry, but you don't need to do that. Can you see there on the monitor – this shot is just on Jennifer? I'm not even in it, so you don't need to worry, thanks anyway . . .'

Five minutes of respite . . . and then jab, jab.

'Hannah. Hannah. We're at lunch, aren't we? Seriously, you don't have to straighten the bow. Thank you anyway . . .'

This went on for days and days and it was driving me nuts.

It got to about day five of filming, and I had a difficult shot to do where I had quite a lot of dialogue to deliver as I walked over the camera tracks laid out on the ground. So, I had to walk and talk simultaneously.

I know . . . . actors are heroes.

The fact was, I had to concentrate. Stephen approached me to discuss the shot and as we were mid-conversation, it started . . . jab, jab, jab at my back. She was at it again.

'Hannah. Sorry, but no, thanks. You don't see the back of me in this shot, so seriously, no. Maybe go and grab a coffee or something? It's fine. Thank you anyway.'

I'd been raised to be polite, even through gritted teeth, but this was pushing me to a sheer edge. She exited. The director finished his notes to me and retreated to his seat by the monitor. At last, I was alone with a few precious moments to gather myself for this tricky shot. Did I know the lines? Would I remember what the director wanted? I heard the camera crew readying themselves for the shot. The call for quiet went up. I took some deep breaths . . .

And it started . . .   Jab, jab, jab.

She was back. Arrived to torture me like a ninja shapeshifter, stealthy and determined. An Exocet missile headed for the middle of my back.

JAB, JAB, JAB.

Chinese water torture.

Drip, drip, drip.

Until – it tipped me.

The top of my skull lifted off and all the devils of hell came rushing out of my mouth. I turned to her, and I hollered in her face,

'The fuckin' bow ISN'T IN THE FUCKIN' SHOT! Get away from me. Or I swear I'll put you closer to your God!'

Poor Hannah's face. I will never forget it. The skin on it was trying to escape, receding backwards. It was as if my yell was amplified like a human leaf-blower. I could see the ripples of shuddering shock undulating across her sweet mush in concentric circles with her little button nose as the centre.

This was the moment I realized that I am a bad, evil, intolerant diva.

Yep, awful.

Look, I know I don't come out well from this story. I'm still ashamed of myself for behaving like that. I'd never done anything like it before, and I've not done anything like it since.

I think it goes to prove that we all have limits.

I often see that awful image of her startled little face in my mind.

I wonder what Hannah is doing now . . . Did she choose to stay in this strange, unpredictable, noisy industry? Perhaps she chose to go elsewhere and work in a calmer and more cordial atmosphere . . . y'know . . . like maybe she works in an abattoir?

Surrounded by screaming pigs. Like me.

Sorry, Hannah, I can't deny it. I was a twat. Perhaps the whole point of reflecting on key moments like this is to reveal to myself some of my hidden fault lines, the places where I might crack if the pressure is high.

Was Hannah annoying? Yes.

Did her fussing warrant the unleashing of the screaming banshee that I apparently can be?

No.

Was I feeling the pressure and vulnerability and fear of performing so, therefore, projected all that on to the nearest sentient being? Probably.

Was it easier to let that happen because the person I let rip on was young, inexperienced and junior? Yes.

Exactly THAT is the reason why it was a twatty thing to do. She was unlikely to push back at me. She was an easy target.

I don't think I considered that in the moment — but I know, on reflection, that it was true. Those circumstances made this one-off minty fit possible, but not right.

Not right at all.

Sometimes shame and twattery belong in the same box.

I have another example of exactly that, but this time it involved two Comic Strip twats.

It happened on a film we made called *Susie*, where I played an over-sexed teacher, a bit of a saucepot.

Just to put it all in context, back in the day the Comic Strip was a really cooperative set-up; we were all very equal. It was a favoured-nations kind of situation, where we were all paid the same, no matter how big or small our roles were. We all wrote/produced/directed the films and it was fantastically inclusive.

Occasionally, as in any democratic organization, there were challenging moments and one of those happened in this film.

Fatty and I were the only women in the central Comic Strip gang and so, of course, we played pretty much all the female parts unless there was a guest. When the two Petes (Richardson and Richens) wrote the films (they wrote most of them), it was very often the case that Jennifer and I played characters who HAPPENED to wear low-cut tops, fishnet tights, fur coats and high heels. Not always, of course, but often enough for us to be on the lookout. This was a typical feminist dilemma. The dichotomy between wanting to be willing and relaxed about playing ANY part – being flattered, frankly, about being considered to play a glamorous role, and not wanting to be an obstructive prude or a killjoy – but, at the same time, listening to your own conscience and keeping your sniffer keen for anything overtly sexist, or silly in an uncomfortable way. The men we worked with were, and still are, our beloved friends. None of them would have had shady intent, but this was the eighties and we were ALL on a steep and sometimes treacherous, always confusing, learning curve about gender perception and equality.

Anyhoo, at the readthrough for this film, the whole Comic Strip contingent were in attendance and it went well, but I had a problem with the very last line of the film. I can't remember it exactly now, but it was something like this. The scene took place in an ambulance and my character Susie had some lines with the handsome doctor:

Susie – Oh, what's your name?

Doc – Kenny.

Susie – Oooh, that's a name to get your lips round.

Something ick like that. I thought it was too obvious and naff and made Susie look cheap in the very last line of a very funny film. I thought that was a shame, so I asked Pete if he would change it. The other Comic Strippers agreed, no big deal, and Pete readily agreed too.

So comes the day of shooting the scene and the rest of the gang aren't there. I look at the script and the bleddy awful line is still there. No prob. It's likely an oversight.

Me – Er, Pete, you said you were going to change this . . . ?

Pete–Yeah,yeah.I'vehadathinkaboutitand,er,Ilikeitsoyoushould say it.

Me – No, that wasn't what we agreed, Pete.

Pete – Yeah, but I want you to say it, so just say it.

Me – No.

Pete – Say it!

Me – . . . right . . .

So, we get into the ambulance. The atmosphere is frosty. The crew undoubtedly sense it. The pressure is on because it's a small space, the end of the afternoon light is fading and the narrow lanes we're filming in are hard to manage with traffic.

Pete shouts, 'Action!'

'Handsome doctor' sits down next to me.

Susie – What's your name?

Doc – Kenny.

I look at him. I don't want to say it.

I turn my head to look out of the window.

I'm not saying it. I decide to smile enigmatically, in a way I know COULD serve as the ending of the film . . .

I hold it. I hold it.

I wait. I wait.

I can feel Pete's eyes boring into me from behind the camera.
Everyone's waiting for me to say that last line. I'm not going to.

I keep smiling.

At long last, after eight years, Pete shouts, 'CUT!'

The ambulance slows down and stops.

Silence.

Pete – Can you step outside for a minute?

Uh oh.

I climb down from the back of the ambulance into the muddy lane
where we've stopped. The inevitable squabble begins with words:

Pete – What the fuck are you doing?!

Me – I'm not saying it.

Pete – Say the line.

Me – Nope, not saying, never will.

Then, suddenly and surprisingly, he shoves me. I push him back. He shoves me again. Push, shove . . . and before I know it, the pair of us descend into a full-on playground fight. It's ridiculous, puerile, preposterous. We might as well be six years old. In fact, a six-year-old would find it childish.

I am so shocked. We are fighting. On the ground. When I stand up, I dust myself down and scowl at Pete, who I despise in this moment, when to my eternal regret, my knee-jerk reaction is to instantly cry. I am so angry and tangled.

Me (through tears) – You can stick your line up your bony arse. I hate you. I wish you were dead.

Pete – Fine. I'd rather die than ever film with you again.

Me – Yeah, well – you're a twat.

Pete – And you are.

Both of us – Twat, twat, twat, twat.

Me – Fine, OK, I'll say the bloody line, then I'm leaving. Good luck with the rest of the filming!

I head back into the ambulance, wiping my eyes and the snot from my nose and straightening up my dress. I resume my seat. It's all very awkward. Pete climbs back in and settles down behind the camera. Here we go . . .

Just as Pete is about to shout for action, the cameraman stops everything . . .

Cameraman – Pete, we can't film. Look at her face. She's all blotchy and there's mascara running down her cheeks. It won't cut in the edit.

Pete looks at me.

Reluctantly, he has to concede and call it a day and we then travel back to the base in silence.

He was then lumbered with only that enigmatic smile as the last shot of the film.

Of course, he hated it, so he cut it short and slapped the titles over it.

I will never forget that ludicrous day.

What a pair of prize twats . . . who are still, to this day, good friends.

AWARD for DESPERATION

FEAT of BORDERLINE RUDENESS

ACHIEVEMENT IN HUBRIS

ATTAINMENT OF WHITE-HOT HUMILIATION

MERIT FOR LOVE ME! NEEDINESS

Performance of Twatness

ARSE-WRENCHING MISTAKES

BEN

'Yes, ladies 'n' gennlemun, little bit o' politics – Thatcher's a monster...'
The gor blimey accent, the sparkly jacket.

One of the big presents the Comic Strip gave me was a lifelong chum in the form of Ben Elton. You seriously can't ask for a more loyal and loving friend. Fact.

This next example of uber twatness involves him and is a mixture of desperation, neediness and hubris – three of my very best qualities.

It's 1990 and Ben has written his first-ever play, which is called *Gasping*. There's a big buzz about it. It's going to open in the West End ... how exciting. We're all wondering who he's going to cast and I'm praying he'll remember his ol' mate 'Dawnie' (that's what he, and he alone, calls me). The thought of being involved in a West End play is entirely thrilling. Being in ANY play, frankly.

I have no idea what the nature of the play is. Gasping? Is it about choking? Or some strange sex games? I care not. I just want to be IN IT, whatever it is. I have no clue if there is even a part in it for which I am suitable. Doesn't matter. Just want to be IN IT.

My giant thirst to be considered is overwhelming. I can't ask him directly. I'm aware that would be massively uncool and compromising for him.

So, I mustn't.

I really mustn't.

I so want to.

Badly want to.

Mustn't.

Must NOT.

NOT...

A few days after hearing about this play, I'm at a mutual friend's house and Ben happens to be there. I'm trying to play it cool, so much so that I'm actively ignoring him in the way that you do when you are HYPER aware of where someone is in a crowded room. My behaviour is odd and, frankly, bordering on rude. I know him well. Why haven't I acknowledged him? Said hello at least? Idiot.

Eventually, he approaches me . . .

Ben – Hi Dawnie. Guess what, I've written a play. Did you know?

Me (casual, dismissive) – Have you? No, I didn't know that. At all. Not heard a peep about it. Nada.

Ben – Yeah, yeah. We're going to open it in the West End in a couple of months, and I want to ask you to play the lead . . .

My breath, all of it, leaves my body, instantly.

OH. MY ACTUAL. GOD!

He's said it. He's just gone and said it just like that. Come out with it. Bold as brass. At a party . . . !

I wobble and stumble slightly. I need to take in breath. Gather myself. Come on, Frenchie.

Me (effusively) – Ben! I can't believe it! My God. I'm so flattered. I'm ecstatic. You total dreamboat. This is WONDERFUL! Thank you, Ben, for putting all your faith in me. I promise I'll bring my A-game for you. Seriously. I love your writing. I won't let you down, mate, you watch. This is just the best news ever. Thank you. Thank you. Thank you.

Ben is looking bemused. He repeats himself for clarity.

Ben – I want to ask HUGH to play the lead. Hugh. Hugh Laurie . . . ?

There is a pause so long I grow a beard.

My stomach is full of concrete.

Shall I just suddenly faint and pretend I'm certifiably deranged? Or that I'm experiencing a *petit mal*? Or dying?

Anything would be preferable to the white-hot humiliation coursing through me right now.

I try to remain calm.

Me (the huge twat) – Of course! Yes, Hugh is a fabulous choice. Good call, Ben. Such a good actor. Yeah. That's definitely who I'd choose if I were you . . . anyway, look, I have to go now, darlin'. There's a taxi waiting . . . to take me directly to hell . . . so . . . bye!

I exit at great speed.

Even the cold night air outside doesn't cool my boiling red face for ages. It's a human baboon's bottom of redness. I need to have my face removed. Sliced off. I can't ever see anyone I know, ever again.

Well . . . the good thing about Ben Elton is that he is such a decent bloke. When he realized I so wanted to be in a play he wrote – he wrote me a play.

It was called *Silly Cow*.

We did it in the West End for eight months.

Phew.

---- ✳ ----

I have form . . . when it comes to bum-clenching mistakes like this.

JAMES BOND

Anyone who knows me knows that technology and I aren't friends. I'm an old-school Luddite. I missed the boat when it came to learning about computers and then I stuck my lil' troglodyte trotters in the mud and resolutely refused to learn the new-fangled machinery of modern life. What a twat. I genuinely believed the internet was a passing phase, a short-lived trend. I decided to wait it out. That was forty or more years ago. It's remarkable how easily pride can infect reason. I have proudly displayed what a technophobic fucknuckle I truly am for this long.

Can I hear a little commotion for my tenacity at least? It is, after all, properly astonishing. Look, am I making life easy for myself resisting all this change? No.

But . . . on the other hand, am I having a more fulfilled and authentic in-the-now life whilst I'm not so distracted by the internet . . . ? Also, no.

Yet again, I excel at being ridiculous.

Anyhoo, I digress. I tell you this about me and technology to give some context to this story.

One of my least favourite offspring of technology is email. I use it, of course, but I genuinely dislike it. It's so perpetually demanding; a continuous cacophony of crap. If you're essentially a polite person like me, the endless email demands require endless email responses, and that's it, your day is gone.

I know, believe me, I know, how lucky I am to have a wonderful PA called Lovely Sue.

That's her official name, by the way.

First name – Lovely.

Surname – Sue.

One of Lovely Sue's jobs is to try and keep all the pestery, rubbishy emails away from me so that I don't service my obedient, dutiful inner sad sap, to the detriment of living my actual life, which I've been known to do. I can disappear into logistical housekeeping and general niceties so frickin' easily, it's frightening. Lovely Sue is a firewall for me. She filters out all the rubbish and sends me little bundles of only the most pertinent emails. So consequently, very few folk have my direct email address and I rarely receive emails that aren't from Lovely Sue.

A while back, she sent me various emails all in one go for my attention, including a very posh invite to the latest Bond film premiere, *No Time to Die*.

These tickets are golden, even in the most ordinary of times, and this film had been delayed twice due to Covid, so this was THE ticket of the year in the movie world. You could regard it as exciting, but I am rubbish at going to red-carpet events like this. Getting a new dress, haircut, posh make-up, thinking of a witty riposte in front of a hundred cameras, trying to avoid looking stunned and trapped. Spending the whole evening suppressing your twatness. Saying something rash and inappropriate, which includes the word 'moist' pertaining to the lead man, which is then reported widely as your only contribution to the evening. Meeting said man soon after and wanting to spontaneously combust rather than lock eyes.

From the minute I say yes to anything like this, the utter dread sets in. I think it's the functioning introvert aspect of me. I'd much rather pay my honest English pounds and go to my local fleapit and break my teeth on unpopped popcorn, to be honest. Lovely Sue knows this about me; she knew I was most likely to say 'no' to this invite.

So, I decided to reply to Lovely Sue in a way that was for her benefit, just to make her laugh. She could then send a proper respectful 'no' on to them afterwards.

I typed the following to Lovely Sue:

```
This will be another big fuck-off red carpet
nightmare, with all the usual utter wankers
in attendance. I'd rather have my eyes pecked
out by diseased pigeons. I'd rather have my
tits munched off by rabid wild dogs, frankly.
So — a polite no from me. Thank you. X
```

I smiled when I pressed 'send'. That would give Lovely Sue a giggle. Tee hee.

IMAGINE MY SURPRISE when, a few moments later, I got a response directly from the posh PR department at the James Bond film . . . to whom I HAD MISTAKENLY SENT THE EMAIL DIRECTLY . . .

Their reply was succinct:

```
Thank you for your speedy response. We
totally understand.
```

AAAAAAAAAAAAAAGH!

How could I have been such a twat?

What a dumb mistake.

There was no elegant way out of it, so I just sent them five hundred emoji laughing faces, in the hope that would somehow cushion the horror.

Yeah. Doubt it.

Doubt they'll ever ask me to anything ever again.

Job done, I guess. Ironically.

OUTSTANDING

There was another moment where Lovely Sue was involved. Oh dear.

Jools Holland is my friend. Sorry to name-drop, but it's a simple fact and has been since we did *The Tube* together in Newcastle in the early eighties.

He was organizing a benefit to raise awareness about prostate cancer. It was to be at the Albert Hall and so he asked me if I would make a quick little twenty-second film on my phone that they could play into the audience on the night and could also be included in the filming of the event for the TV broadcast. He was asking lots of other chums to do the same, not just me.

Now, I am asked quite often to do this sort of thing – little quick supports or endorsements, etc. If I decide to do it, I try and wait to do a few together when I have washed my hair, put on lipstick and look vaguely like a female human. Normally, I film them quickly on my phone and ping them off.

Anyway, I'd had a chaotically busy couple of weeks and for a moment, I couldn't remember if I'd done this little film for Jools or not.

I said to Lovely Sue, 'Can you just call Jools' people and ask if I've done that little film?'

She called me back and said, 'It's outstanding.'

I was delighted.

I went into a monologue,

'Aww, is it? Thanks for saying that, Sue, cos, y'know, I do a lot of these things and you never know if people really like them or not, so I appreciate that. I do try my hardest to keep the standards up if I can...'

She interrupted me.

'No, Dawn ... it's outstanding – as in YOU HAVEN'T DONE IT YET.'

Right.

Ah.

So, I was busy lapping up the credit for an OUTSTANDING twenty-second film about prostate cancer, bathing in the praise for a film I HADN'T MADE YET.

Hubris much?

Prime twat.

ROYAL TWATTERY

I have told the story before about the time the Queen Mother came for tea at our house when I was very tiny.

I know, right?

It was a huge moment for our little family. I was so delighted when, for a show I did a few years back, *30 Million Minutes*, we managed to track down some archive footage of this remarkable incident.

There she is, resplendent in lilac, walking up our garden path for all to see.

There we are: handsome, young, uniformed dad; nervous, beautiful, young mum; newly shorn and Brylcreemed brother; and paralysed with shock right down to my new shiny-red Clarks Start-Rite shoes me.

It was a bit traumatic for a four-year-old, to be honest. The Queen Mother did NOT wear a crown. She did NOT arrive in a carriage pulled by unicorns, and when she smiled, she had brown teeth, which were alarming at the least and beyond terrifying at the most. I couldn't believe that my family were willingly allowing a patent witch into our home. I hid from her and had nothing to say when she spoke to me. Unusual behaviour for a tiny show-off who was ordinarily an incessant blabbermouth.

When I lived in Cyprus as a six-year-old (my dad was posted there with the RAF), my grandparents sent a radio request for me on BFPO radio. The presenter said, 'This next song is for a little girl called Dawn French, are you there, Dawn...?'

I genuinely believed the radio was talking to me (junior twat), so replied feebly, 'Yes.' The presenter continued, 'Good' (confirmed it). 'Well, your grandma and grandad know you are a chatterbox, so this one is for you. It's "Happy Talk" from the musical South Pacific... *' That's how much my family knew I was a yapper.*

My parents couldn't believe that I clammed up as soon as I laid eyes on Her Majesty. I clung to my father's leg with the determination of a randy terrier the entire time she was with us. I was a human boot he was wearing, having to heave me along as he showed her around our small house. Despite the loaded 'looks' I was undeniably getting from them, signalling that I should stop this ludicrous behaviour, I persisted until she left. I think they laughed it off as 'silly' and 'cute', but it was early onset twat, no doubt.

That was my very first encounter with a Royal. You would think that perhaps I might learn from it, wouldn't you? Learn how to behave in a less embarrassing way should I ever come face to face with a Royal in the future . . . ?

Yeah. Think again.

Fatty Saunders and I were invited to the Women of the Year lunch once. It's an extraordinary event, crammed to the rafters with women who are leaders in their various fields. There are pilots and priests and politicians and on and on. Impressive women, getting together to celebrate their achievements. It's a giant ballroom bursting with potent oestrogen, and it's properly awe-inspiring.

The sound of this room as you approach is a curiously odd experience. The room is full of formidable people, but it sounds like a giant aviary of twittering budgies. It's such a shocking contradiction. I suppose it's because there are no balancing bass tones of men in the mix. It's pure high pitch. Unforgettable.

We were flattered to be asked, and even more surprised when, on entering the main room, we were hived off into a VIP area. It was strange. We were in exactly the same room as everyone else, but we were inside a red-velvet roped-off pen. Like distinguished cattle. If anything, we were rather crammed in, so it was an awkward crush. A cage full of elite heifers, being corralled and controlled until the right moment.

This side of the rope – prize stock.
That side of the rope – common stock.

It was so very silly. We were trying to talk to various friends outside the rope, but the guard was determinedly guarding us so that we shouldn't venture out of our category.

Anyway, back in the day, they loved to have a Royal to bless this lunch. On this one occasion, it was Fergie, who later gave us a talk about 'Harmony', which was . . . edifying.

I like Sarah Ferguson. Anytime I've ever come across her, she is utterly jolly and keen to engage in that winning way that only posh girls can. You sort of get swept along with the irrepressibly blousy confidence of it all and, before you know it, you've been completely charmed.

The organizers were fussing about, making sure we were all lined up correctly to greet her – the guest of honour. They had us all in a line, like sausages sizzling in a pan, ready to formally receive and respect her. Now look, I'm a fan of the Royal Family. I like all the history and pomp and tradition and costumes and weddings and castles and crowns and all that ... but I don't think they are a superior race or something. Quite the opposite – these poor buggers don't get to choose much at all. Their lives are mapped out, like it or not, and they have zero privacy. On the other hand, they get tons of presents and own some of the best art and houses and land in the world. However institutionalized, they are human people in the end. The ones I've met have been completely lovely and very good at their jobs – meaning they make a proper effort to be sociable and interested in twats like me. I'm pretty sure that under all the ermine and diamonds they are also glorious twats. We know this, don't we? It's THE MAIN thing I like about them; perhaps the ONLY relatable aspect. They make mistakes, they fall out, they hold resentments, they get hurt and jealous and irritated. Like me. Like you.

They do stupid stuff. Like me. Like you.

They have DREADFUL relatives who've done DREADFUL stuff. Like me. Like you. They are embarrassed and awkward. Like me. Like you.

As our premier family though, they are held to a higher standard than all of us. Not like me. Not like you.

That part might require us to wrap some understanding around it in the long run, I think, if they are to survive in their present form.

So, back to the Women of the Year lunch. Fatty and I had had a chat beforehand about the protocol when meeting a Royal. If I remember rightly, there was a little reminder sent alongside the invite with a few key points to guide us. I can't recall EXACTLY, but there were things like:

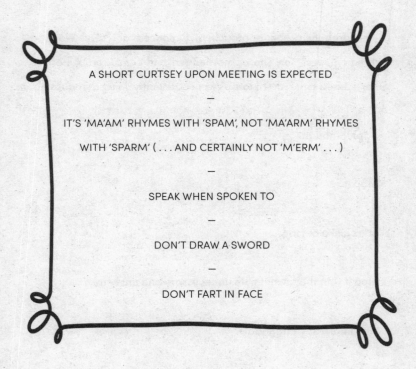

A SHORT CURTSEY UPON MEETING IS EXPECTED

—

IT'S 'MA'AM' RHYMES WITH 'SPAM', NOT 'MA'ARM' RHYMES

WITH 'SPARM' (. . . AND CERTAINLY NOT 'M'ERM' . . .)

—

SPEAK WHEN SPOKEN TO

—

DON'T DRAW A SWORD

—

DON'T FART IN FACE

. . . that sort of thing, but more formal.

Both of us agreed that the whole shebang was archaic and preposterous. We would be respectful, of course, but we wouldn't kowtow to these ridiculously outdated rituals. The furthest we were prepared to go was a dignified quick and minimal nod of the head. That would do, we decided. We were adult women meeting another adult woman, for heaven's sake; let's just keep it on the down-low and real, shall we? Let's not be complicit in the bowing and scraping nonsense.

As Sarah Ferguson approached, I glanced at Fatty. We're in agreement, yes? Yes, she acknowledged and concurred. All of the other women in the row before us were obediently doing as requested.

Saps, I thought.

Stop it.

She's just a person.

Stop it with the fawning. It's unnecessary and unseemly.

Silly. Ludicrous. Laughable.

We were next. I was first, before Fatty. Sarah Ferguson put her alabaster, game head-girl hand out for me to shake . . . at which point, I was suddenly possessed by some kind of dutiful convention devil.

I buckled to my knee in a deep, deep, disgusting display of revolting deference the like of which any arse-licking courtier in Versailles might have aspired to. I don't know what happened. I was struck by celestial Royal lightning or something. The exaggerated reverence was shameful.

The sheer over-veneration of it. Awful. Bowing. Scraping. Why couldn't I stop? I could see that some of the other women were laughing. Maybe they thought for a moment that it was a joke? It wasn't. It was full-on sycophancy.

I was actually genuflecting, exhibiting tons more worship than I felt. What the hell was wrong with me? Did I think I'd be beheaded if I didn't behave this way? I was bobbing so furiously that you'd be forgiven for mistaking me for one of those dippy drinking birds who are stuck to your glass and dunk their beaks repeatedly into your Pimm's. I was trapped in a repeated cycle of perpetual toad. I couldn't have been more disgusted with myself. I paused from one of many deep bows to see that, mercifully, she had moved on. Fatty was next and she would surely hold firm, resist the urge to ingratiate herself. She's much more resolute than me . . .

But no.

She succumbed. Same.

Not quite as creepy as me, not so bendy, but full curtsey with swords, medals and spurs-type stuff. Fairly revolting.

Once we'd blown sufficient unctuous smoke up her bum, Sarah Ferguson was free to move on graciously.

Lord only knows what impression she had of the pair of us.

We didn't know who or what we were either.

Except a pair of revoltingly toadying dolts.

Something about the presence of Royalty is unnerving; you get swept along by their importance and forget yourself. If this is true for most people, the Royals must spend a lot of their time meeting disingenuous, giggling idiots like us.

I let myself down on yet another occasion when, in 2005, I voiced the character of Mrs Beaver opposite Ray Winston as Mr Beaver in *The Lion, the Witch and the Wardrobe* in the Narnia series of films. Obviously, since the characters were animated, we didn't need to turn up on the set but, of course, we were expected to turn up at the Royal Premiere of the film, which was a huge, sparkly red-carpet affair at the Albert Hall. I took my family with me, and they were all waiting patiently in their seats whilst Ray and I joined Tilda Swinton, James

McAvoy, Jim Broadbent and the rest of the stellar cast in the line-up to meet Prince Charles and Camilla.

I've met Charles several times and I really like the cut of his particular jib. He has a cheek that I warm to (and the other one ain't so bad either!). He came to see a production of *A Midsummer Night's Dream* in which I played Bottom, the mechanical, and was very chipper and encouraging to the whole cast and, what's more, evidenced a startling knowledge of Shakespeare. I don't know why that surprised me; the bloke's had a decent education. I just find it heartening when prominent folk are passionate about the Arts.

Anyhoo – back to the future King. And me.

I'm in the line, all dolled up and ready to meet the very important peoples.

As with any line like this, he stops to speak to everyone, so the anticipation and panic have time to build to almost uncontrollable levels. Ray and I are messing about, whispering to each other as we wait our turn.

Me (to Ray) – I'm thinking I might just lift up my top and show him my baps . . .

Ray – That's perfectly appropriate.

Me – There are cameras; the evening news are here.

Ray – Ideal. Captured for all posterity . . . show yer bum, then it can also be for all posteriority.

We are giggling like schoolkids. I can tell that my hysteria levels are rising. I'm far too excited for my own good.

The Royals are talking to the producers, the director, other cast members. Prince Charles is first; Camilla is right behind him. He's getting closer. My heart is pounding a bit faster; here he comes . . .

Then . . .

He arrives at me. He's right in front of me. I've stupidly forgotten what I'm supposed to do curtseying-wise.

I mustn't repeat the Sarah Ferguson catastrophuk.

I dally with the idea of curtseying but reject it at the last minute, which somehow morphs into an awkward sway. He must surely think I'm drunk.

I can't remember his opening line to me, but it's something charming and generic like:

'How are you?'

For some gobsmacking reason, I decide to reply with only wide-eyed gurning and high-pitched giggling. I've become a simpleton. It's completely odd. I'm already slightly out of control, primed and pumped for mischief.

I have to preface what happened next with the irrefutable fact that HE started it . . . Miss!

In an effort to staunch my giggle-fest, I suspect, he says to me:

'The last time we met, I saw your Bottom . . .'

Cheeky Prince! This tickles me.

I should have left it at that; let him have the last, funny, word.

But no.

I'm Dawney-go-too-far, aren't I?

I rashly decide to chance it . . .

So I reply, 'Yes. And tonight, Sir,
you will see my Beaver . . . '

I hear Ray Winston's sharp intake of horrified breath next to me.

The world stops turning for a moment. The Prince and I lock eyes.
There's a long, treacherous pause, where I realize I'm off to the Tower
for head removal purposes.

Not only have I been potty-mouthed crude, but I've also trumped
his rather good joke. This is raw treason, surely?

I'd kill me if I were Queen. He has every right. It would be correct.

But no – he is dignified. He smiles politely and moves swiftly on.

Phew.

Yes, I've been a twat, but I seem to have gotten away with it.

I am SO BUSY watching him move down the line, eyes glued to him deftly greeting all the rest, mesmerized by him and somewhat pole-axed by my own idiocy, that I am rendered deaf for a minute . . .

In my overwhelming desire to eat my words, and consumed with giant regret, I don't hear the female voice in my ear:

'Hello? Dawn?'

As I jerk out of my reverie, I'm actually irritated, so I yell, 'What?!' as I turn to see Camilla standing right in front of me, waiting patiently for me to notice her.

Shit! How rude of me.

So, I launch into a babble of excuses:

Me – God, sorry, I was just telling him (HIM?!?!) about my beaver? NO! God, no, that sounds wrong. Never mind. Shush now. Me, I mean, not you. God, no. Sorry. Here we go. Best to move along. Thank you. Curtsey (I do). Off with my head. Goodbye and thank you for coming . . .

By now, she has wandered off. Why stick around to hear more incoherent, cretinous blether from a lunatic...?

And there, ladies and gentlemen, was where I left all dignity on the carpet. Marvellously twatty.

A further curious Royal encounter occurred when Jennifer and I took part in a benefit for the Benesh Institute, who are a centre of excellence in the world of dance/movement notation. It looks like music on a page and dancers can read it like notes – it's amazing. At the time, Princess Margaret was the main patron and she was there on this auspicious night at the Royal Opera House in Covent Garden.

This was one of those times when our job in comedy brought us together with remarkable people to create an unforgettable experience that would've been the stuff of dreams for junior Dawn many years before. Jennifer and I together have had several mind-blowing moments like this, e.g.:

- WORKING WITH MEMBERS OF MONTY PYTHON AND PETER COOK AT BENEFITS LIKE THE SECRET POLICEMAN'S BALL

- MAKING A CHART-TOPPING SINGLE WITH THE SPICE GIRLS WITH OUR OWN GIRL BAND LANANEENEENOONOO

- WORKING ALONGSIDE UB40, BILLY BRAGG AND THE PRETENDERS AT ENDLESS ANTI-RACISM BENEFITS AND RALLIES

These are the times you get up close and personal with people you love and admire; when you can pretend, for a while at least, that you are all bestie mates; when you address Paul McCartney with 'Hi Mate!' at a 'do' – as if he's a human rather than A BEATLE! Admittedly, he immediately takes out a restraining order on you but, hey, it was worth it to have a single incident of casual banter with him . . .

So, this particular evening was star-studded with all the great and graceful of the ballet and dance world, and we were sharing a dressing room with the elite.

To my astonishment, the gold star on the door announced the occupants:

Miss Darcey Bussell
Miss Sylvie Guillem
Miss Viviana Durante
Miss Jennifer Saunders
Miss Dawn French

This was, and probably still is, one of 'those' moments where I had to blink to be sure it was real. We were prima ballerinas. Well, pretend ones, for one night only.

We were there to do a silly sketch, of course. We'd had Darcey on *French and Saunders* before to join in some ballet nonsense we cooked up. On this particular night, we were to do a little dance where I was to be Darcey's reflection in a cheeky routine with tutus and a huge mirror. It was something we later reprised in *Vicar of Dibley*, but this was its incarnation, its debut. Jennifer was playing a bossy dance teacher who carried a cane, chain-smoked and kept shouting instructions to 'Good toes! Naughty toes!'

It was a hoot to both take part and also to watch so many wonderful dancers from side-stage. We had been asked to provide alternative costumes for the walk-down at the end, so I asked a friend to make me a preposterous outfit where I looked like an old-fashioned formal ballerina in a pink tutu, sitting astride a huge swan – a bit like Bernie Clifton used to do when he was riding his ostrich back in the day.

So, my actual legs were the swan's legs with black tights and huge black flippers on the feet. And there were silly little thin pink fake legs hanging down astride the big papier-mâché swan. It looked suitably ridiculous, and luckily there was a big laugh, so – job done.

As the final curtain came down, the stage manager told us to wait on the stage because Princess Margaret was coming down from the Royal Box to give us all a Royal blessing.

Her Royal Highness knew a lot about ballet, it seems, and she spoke at length to all the fantastic dancers.

I was a bit nervous. I was massively aware that I looked odd, what with the giant swan wrapped around me, 'n'all. Eventually, she arrived in front of us. I over-smiled at her, utilizing ALL of my teeth, as trained. There was the strangest look in her eyes, which I recognized as full-on pity. She leaned in and quietly whispered two of the most devasting words I'd ever heard . . .

'How brave.'

To which, of course, I answered, 'Yes, thank you.' As if she were right.

I have no idea what was going on in her head, or mine for that matter, but I suspect she genuinely believed that I was a bit 'special' and possibly 'challenged'. Bloody cheek! How dare she? I waddled back to my star-studded dressing room and caught sight of myself in the mirror – a full-length twat looking back at me. She wasn't far wrong.

HUBRIS OR VANITY?

I might have remained in Cornwall as a young person if there had been a university here the like of Falmouth University today. It has become one of the leading Arts establishments in the country. It's honestly SO IMPRESSIVE. I can't quite get my head around the quality of the resources there, from TV studios to animation studios, from sprung-floor dance studios to music studios. And there are TONS of spaces that AREN'T studios! The huge campus, or several campuses (what's the plural? – I dunno) are in the most beautiful part of the country. In one year, I remember, Fal Uni came third in the world for an award voted for by students to do with how fast a student could physically get from lecture hall to riding a wave shouting 'cowabunga!' In Falmouth, it's something like seven minutes. The Uni came third, after Hawaii and California!

In 2015, my great friend (who I trust not to throw me to the wolves or waste my time in any way) Michael Grandage, a fantastic director who is an honorary fellow at Falmouth, approached me on behalf of the Uni to become their first-ever Chancellor. Although the art school was founded in 1902, it didn't receive university status until 2013.

I'm sure this kind of prominent position is desirable to plenty o' folk. Some people love all the pomp and palaver. Some people are easy-going and light-hearted about it all, take it in their stride. I am not. I'm a functioning introvert, which, as I interpret it, means that I absolutely CAN be around lots of people, put myself in the spotlit heart of things and draw public attention to myself, BUT I'm not fond of it. It's not my natural happy place so, in order to do it, I have to prepare and psych myself up. Plus, when it's done, I conk out exhausted. I know all this about myself. I know it now. For many years, I didn't work it out. I went to parties and dinners and 'dos' and couldn't work out why being around tons of people left me feeling wretched. I don't do well. I over-back-think it, whatever it is. I regret moments if, for instance, I know there are people I didn't get to see or, worse, if I manage to spend time with a beloved and then someone annoying demands my attention in the distance behind their heads. It's all too tricky for me to navigate without seeming massively rude or distracted.

All of this is to say that when Michael came to me with this request to take on the job of Chancellor, I really didn't want to put myself centre stage like that. Plus, honestly, I had no idea what the position entailed and I didn't want to commit to something so important when I knew full well I wouldn't have the proper time to give it. I seem to live in a state of perpetual guilt about all the charities/organizations/projects I'm involved with that I can't give time to.

I want a fermata.

I want to stop time so that I can catch up.

I'm pretty sure that when my time comes to meet my maker, I won't actually have time to die. I'll be too busy trying to sort out everything I've been negligent of. Dying will have to wait until I've tidied up my life and put a full stop on every email, text, letter and tweet.

Basically, I knew that it was utterly the wrong time for me to take on yet another commitment. I didn't care to disappoint more people, which I surely would if I accepted.

I was pretty resolute.

No. It's too public. Too showy. No.

Michael persuaded me to at least have dinner with the then Vice-Chancellor Professor Anne Carlisle and various trustees and members of the board. I don't know why I agreed to that part because it's so much harder to stand your own ground when you are face to face.

As usual, the lure of:

1) free food

2) Falmouth

3) free food

and, most importantly . . .

4) free food

is what swung it. I took my husband along with me for supportive ballast, only to discover that he was the biggest turncoat since that bloke they named a volte-face after, what was his name? Oh yes – **Judas**.

On the way in:

Me – Right, I need to say a speedy and firm no to this. Obviously not 'til we've had the main course. Somewhere mid-pudding is my cunning plan, and you'll support me, right?

Husband – Count on it.

Me – Plus, I don't want to stay too late, so can you hoick me outta there around nine-thirty p.m.? Make up something if you have to. Say your pacemaker is failing . . .

Husband – I don't have a pacemaker.

Me – I know that, but they don't . . .

Husband – I don't want to lie.

Me – OK, well . . . say you're called away suddenly. Your beeper's gone off – on important secret MI5 business . . .

Husband – Right.

Me – And don't let me agree to this. I categorically DON'T want to do it, OK?

Husband – OK.

We went in and sat down.

It didn't help that everyone there was delightful. I was hoping they'd be on one end or the other of the academic spectrum. Either so fustily unrelatable or so hippily whacky that I could easily run away guilt-free. But no, it seemed that Falmouth Uni had a group of clever, funny, interesting and dynamic folk leading it on into change and a really exciting-sounding future.

All of that was tempting, but no, I must stand firm.

Then they described the new ideas they had to develop a business hub to launch innovative projects the students came up with. Converting degrees into actual jobs. Jobs that the students themselves create.

All of that was tempting, but no, I must stand firm.

Then they told me about the bursaries they offer local Cornish students to encourage them to stay in their own county and take advantage of the opportunities on their doorstep.

All of that was tempting, but no, I must stand firm.

Then they told me the Uni was ranked first among Arts universities that year.

No. 1!! All of that was tempting, but no, I must stand firm.

Then they reminded me of the fact that the creative industries are driving growth in the UK, and how much of a revenue-earner the fashion industry is, and how well-equipped the fashion and textile department at the Uni is. As is the gaming and animation department . . .

. . . and the film school.

And the architecture arm of the Uni.

And the photography.

And the TV studies.

And music.

And dance.

All of that was tempting, but no, I must stand firm.

Then my husband openly said:

'Blimey, it sounds AMAZING!'

Judas.

He wasn't wrong, but that wasn't the point. We were supposed to be a united front. He knew the plan of action. What a heinous betrayal.

He then tag-teamed-up with Michael to start trying to persuade me. Unbebleddylievable!

No, I must stand firm.

I've already decided it would be a vainglorious move for me. It's too 'shiny' a role. I'm a reluctant celeb. I avoid all the attention-seeking stuff . . . don't I?

Yeah, this is the story I told myself, and I was very nearly believing it until the conversation turned to the ceremonial gowns and caps. I was reminded of the amazing day my own mum received an honorary degree in Plymouth. She was so proud and she was invited to give a speech on the podium, which was extremely rousing — except for the fact that, swamped in all the giant, voluminous academic gear including the bonnet-style cap, my diminutive mother looked for all the world like some kind of Tudor hobbit, so I couldn't take her at all seriously. She was also ENTIRELY hidden behind the lectern and the microphone was positioned for someone lofty, so it was way above her head. She was a living, whispering Diddyman.

I started to engage in a conversation about how much I disliked all that preposterous gear, and it occurred to me that in such a creative establishment, why wouldn't the fashion students themselves design an outfit for a new Chancellor?

This chance musing was immediately accepted as a good idea and I started to be drawn in, imagining the nature of such a gown, custom-made, bespoke, glorious.

In the very next instant, it happened.

Probably the most avaricious sudden desire I've ever had. I should have kept it well inside, but I didn't. I put it out in the air for all to hear when I suddenly blurted out:

'Hey, can I have a crown?'

All eyes on me. They are a bit startled, but I push on, like a greedy human magpie.

'And maybe a big chunky chain, y'know, like proper regalia? And a big fuck-off brooch? Real bling. Huge . . . bling.

'Can I have that if I say yes?'

Somewhat cornered, Anne readily agreed, and there and then, for the craven love of a bit of plush, I sold my hollow soul. It wasn't about the university, the students, education, Cornwall or any of the honourable stuff.

It was about jewellery.

What a twat.

Of course, it's important to add that since that unguarded, rather revealing and, frankly, unsavoury declaration, I have taken the actual job of the job rather more seriously for the last eight years. In fact, it has become a joy to be involved in the evolution of a new university, learning how it works and witnessing the challenges, the achievements and the dynamism of such a place. I was so touched by the way the university and the faculty adapted to all the changes that Covid brought. How on earth could students learn any of the Arts remotely? By remarkable and innovative teaching, that's how.

I could blether on about it ad nauseam, but suffice to say that I don't regret saying yes for a second.

For the record – the students did indeed design my robe, helped, of course, by their skilled teachers. It's a silk and cotton damask with Cornish flowers and ferns woven into it. There are beautiful iridescent black beads on the hem to signify the wings of the Cornish chough. The inside has a Cornish tartan for a lining, and there are two secret (not now!) ribbons that hang down my back, on which there are embroidered the names of each student who took part in its creation, sewn by their own hands. It's unusual and wonderful and not at all stuffy and I love it. I have worn it to give every student their degree at graduation since 2015.

As for the bling . . .

Well.

The MAGNIFICENT Falmouth-based jeweller Mirri Damer designed a matching crown and brooch (we ditched the chain when I realized how clunky and heavy it would be) for me. God – it is breathtaking. She used the phrase 'blasted heath', which so well describes the windswept trees along the rugged Cornish coast, as her inspiration. She set the gold leaf crown with tiny shells and serpentine, which is a Cornish semi-precious stone found on the Lizard. The same for the brooch – worn over my heart.

This crown, too, is worn to give out every single degree. It's so precious I have to wear white gloves to handle it.

I love it.

I love it.

I love it.

Even though I know it was appropriated in such a greedy, naughty way.

I still love it.

I get to wear a crown for dogs' sake!

Who do I think I am?

Chancellor?

Oh, wait . . . yes, I am. Proudly and happily.

Representing excellent education in the county I love.

Was it vanity? Yep.

Was it hubris? Yep.

Do I care? Nope.

Am I a twat? Yep. Big time.

Do I care? Nope.

Do I secretly wish I could bring the crown home and wear it round the house in my slippers? You bet.

ELTON JOHN

I've made it clear that I'm not the person to invite to a party. I dread them.

But . . .

There are always exceptions in life, times when you ought to say yes, however uncomfortable, because the experience will be unforgettable. For whatever reason.

In my life, the reason, the only reason, to go to a big, glittery party is – Elton John.

I know.

Clang. I've dropped a big shiny name, just like that.

Somehow, somewhere along the way, I came into the orbit of Elton John. I can't even remember exactly when or how now, but gradually I came to realize that we sorta knew each other well enough to hug whenever we met. It seemed to be a step up from that strange celebby mutual recognition thing that goes on. I've never really understood the rules of that. I would hope that surely the basic ground rules are to generally be kind and friendly to anyone you meet, whether they are famous or not? There's a different level, though, that kicks in when you see someone you know because of their music or acting or whatever their public work is. You don't know them at all, of course, but you can't help it. You do a big acknowledging nod and a little 'hello, yes, I know who you are' wave. The unwritten rule is that the recipient of this generosity reciprocates in kind with an equal, if not more expansive, gesture of recognition and approval. 'Yes, I know you too, and I like you.' It can end there or it can burgeon into a lifelong mutual love or anything in between. Typical of the common or garden British celeb, the manners and etiquette surrounding this odd little ritual are crucial to get right. It's an intricate code, a dainty dance. You need to learn the choreography. Doing it even a bit wrong can land you in celeb jail very easily or, at the very least, lead you to being shunned and excluded from all sparkly things for a time. Woe betide you if you don't catch that particular singer's eye at the correct moment. He will forever accuse you of 'blanking' him, even though you didn't have your specs on and you genuinely didn't see him. I name no names. But honestly, that grudge has been held since 1984 and no amount of snivelling arse-licking ever since to make up for it seems to work. You can come a cropper very easily. It's a showbiz minefield, daaaahling. Ugh. You see, this is the sort of stuff I can't be doing with, but somehow I'm drawn into the dreadful dance ...

One of the best moments in my life EVER was in this category of 'what to do when you see someone famous that you admire'. It was the early eighties and I was at a party at the Wag Club in Soho. I think it was something to do with Elvis Costello – an album launch or something? Anyhoo, I spotted Alison Moyet. I was, still am, a huge fan, and so I felt a bit giddy. I so wanted to meet her but was a bit nervous to approach. She looked at me from across the room and immediately started to imitate a dance I'd done in a Comic Strip film. Oh my God. She's seen a film I'm in, and she's teasing me with it! Heaven. I responded with my version of it. She did more moves. I did more moves. We were flirting outrageously. It was bliss. Eventually, we spoke and I'm happy to report that we've been beloveds ever since. Of the highest order. Through thick and thin. True love. So – parties ain't all bad …

So – sorry – back to Elton John. Where were we …?

He is the undisputed King of the glamorous party, so however reluctant I might feel to go, his parties are SOMETHING ELSE. He used to host one every year in his house and gardens near Windsor, called The White Tie and Tiara Ball. All funds would go to his various AIDS charities and it was THE party of the year.

I always fretted about what to wear, but in the end, it never mattered. These parties had the best entertainers on stage. No one says no to Elton, it seems. The food, the décor, the settings, the music, the people – these are nights I will never forget, and here follows a few memory slices that stay with me:

- Holding Kate Winslet in my arms, both of us quite (very) drunk, and each of us crying and whispering, 'No, YOU are the best one of all,' in turn to each other (we've hardly met).

- Watching Richard Gere (I know) actively try to chat up Princess Diana (!), who was clearly flattered, but having none of it . . . until I felt the need to extricate her from the situation (who do I think I am?) by sidling up next to her and claiming, 'I'm from Rescue a Princess. I believe you made a request by dint of an internal scream . . . ?'

Luckily, she laughed. Otherwise, I could've mistakenly been heading off one of the most exciting love stories of the century. Imagine what those potential extra Princes would've been like! What a saucy story it would all make. I'm sure she spent a deal of time batting away overkeen wannabe paramours. She was, up close and in her lovely skin, REALLY beautiful. I can't claim to have known her properly, but in those few minutes, we were chuckling chums, like any ol' girlfriends, and her willingness to misbehave a bit appealed massively to me.

It did occur to me in that moment that Richard Gere MIGHT have hoped that a lil' 'liaison' with our Princess could well lead to him becoming King . . . maybe?

- Diana did tell me a funny little thing. She said that she'd been watching a kid's film (Disney, maybe?) that started with a prince throwing open the curtains in his castle and the narrator commenting, 'And the Prince knew that one day when the old King died, he would be the ruler of all he surveyed as far as the eye could see . . .'

She said that her small son mumbled at the TV, 'Yeah? So?'

She laughed so much when she told me this, and I warmed to her even more. A mother enjoying her tiny son's hilarious (and admittedly rather rare) musings on life.

- I remember a heated moment between the wonderful actor Jimmy Nail and the renowned acerbic TV critic A.A. Gill. Jimmy clearly had historic beef with Gill, who had apparently insulted Jimmy by commenting rudely about his face. Jimmy has an extraordinary face, of course he does; he's an extraordinary person with extraordinary talents. Gill had disparaged his face. Jimmy quietly reminded Gill that his face, his features, were his inheritance from his beloved parents and that Gill had no right to criticize them, and that Jimmy took it personally. Jimmy has never been afraid of a necessary confrontation, and he certainly wouldn't lie down and be bullied by ANYONE. He invited Gill outside to resolve the issue. I have never seen a man quite so terrified, or with skin as pale as Gill's, as he duly followed orders to 'continue the conversation' outside the party. Nothing much happened, of course, it was enough that Jimmy scared him. Jimmy told me that apparently Gill requested him, ironically, to 'leave the face alone' when he thought he was about to get a pounding . . .

- I also remember hearing for the first time the fantastic Anastacia sing, which totally blew my mind and led to Jennifer and me asking her to come and join us on *French and Saunders* to do a sketch, which became a key moment for me, but more of that anon . . .

All of these moments, and so many more, were moments that stayed with me from the fab parties at Elton John's. He is the undisputed King of parties, and I don't say no.

For his fiftieth, he threw a huge, lavish fancy dress party at the Hammersmith Palais. He really pushed the boat out this time and arrived in a removal van that could accommodate his giant Versailles-style wig, his husband David (also dressed to the nines) and a few sexy flunkeys to boot. What an entrance. So very understated – not!

The first Mr French (a bloke called Len) and I were absolutely delighted when we were invited to this party. Thrilled.

But – of course – oh dear . . .

There were those two dreadful words on the posh invite: 'Fancy Dress'.

Oh Lord. I don't know about you, but these words fill me with sick. I can't get it right; I don't know why.

There are seasoned partygoers, y'know, elegant, sophisticated people who get the memo about this. For them, it's a cinch, a chance to dress up and come out to play.

They understand the requirements.

The outfit needs to:

- be glamorous

- look good on the red carpet

- be effortlessly chic

- be marvellously comfortable

- be suitable to be danced in

Every single other guest at this high-profile party got it right.

Not us. Oh no, no, no.

For some reason that only Satan knows, we decided to go as Michael Jackson and his pet chimp Bubbles.

Why? For the love of all that's holy – WHY?!

Don't ask me.

One of the worst decisions of my life. Along with getting a curly perm.

And getting a Komodo dragon as a pet (that bit is a lie).

I think it was because Len already had a Michael Jackson outfit hanging about in the garage from some ol' sketch or other.

So, we were halfway there with the outfit.

Len also . . . wait for it . . . decided to go in WHITE FACE.

WHAAAAT!!!??!!

It's so unthinkable now.

But, in his defence, Michael Jackson himself (coincidentally exactly the same age as Len) was in white face at the time.

But still . . . dear God . . . regrettable.

However bad his decision was – and it was indeed very, very, fucky bad – it was seriously nothing on mine.

I called up my friend Pat who used to make costumes for us last minute for *French and Saunders* and is unfazed by any bizarre request.

Me – Pat, can you quickly make me an adorable little chimpanzee outfit, y'know, with a sweet little head, cute ears. I'll get one of those plastic monkey faces to slot in, with the little pinpricks for eyes so I can see . . . ?

So off she went and started on it. She's mighty quick.

I was very busy at the time and didn't have time for a fitting.

RED FLAG!

I went along to her studio and as I went to take the outfit off the rail, it fell to the floor like a sack of nails, it was SO HEAVY.

Darlin' Pat had decided to use the thickest, the densest nylon fur fabric she could find. Not only that, but she'd lined it with a lovely quilted woollen lining . . . which would have been perfect if this party had been in the North Pole.

It wasn't.

It was in the very hot Hammersmith Palais.

So – the day of the party comes, we get all dressed up. We've hired a chauffeur with a posh car to take us the twenty miles or so from our house.

We're sitting in the back of the car in all the gear. I have made a strange decision to put everything that would ordinarily be in a handbag (chimpanzees don't have handbags, you idiot!) down my pants for ease. I have keys, perfume, gum, the invite, snacks, etc., all in my pants.

As we travel the half-hour or so, I'm starting to sweat profusely.

It's hot.

It's hot.

It's really hot.

I'm suffering from heat exhaustion and we're not even there yet!

This is very bad news.

There is the distinct whiff of my own rotting flesh escaping up through the neck hole of my outfit and wafting into my nostrils.
Oh God.

I'm actually decomposing.

We arrive at the party. I'm still alive, but only just. We climb out of the car on to the red carpet and I'm thinking, 'Well, look, we've come this far, made all this effort, we have to go in, although I'd really much rather be going straight to hospital.'

I take the hand of my weird white-faced Michael Jackson husband, and I decide to go all in with the monkey impression, so I give it the full apey-gait, including chimp noises, all the way up the red carpet. The *Planet of the Apes* casting director would be on the phone to my agent in a hot instant, it's so darn accurate.

I'm giving it full-on monkey as we approach Elton and David, who are greeting everyone arriving. I can't see through the pinpricks very well, but they both look impressive. They also look a bit confused, and quite alarmed.

They clearly have absolutely no idea who we are.

Len doesn't look like Len.

I don't look like me.

We are totally unrecognizable.

Nobody knows who we are.

I don't even know who we are any more.

Security guards move forward and quickly usher us past Elton and David into the party, so we don't even say hello.

The minute we get into the heaving party, I lean in to Len:

Me – I'm on the verge of death in here; we need to go.

So, we walk straight to the back door, get back into the same car and race home.

Total number of minutes at the party = FOUR.

I was panting for breath in the car and when we finally arrived home, I could at last take the bloody awful thing off.

It flumped to the floor with a squelch — because it contained ALL of my body fluids. I stood there in my soaking wet industrial bra and pants as all my 'handbag' goods flopped to the ground in a congealed heap. All except my keys, which had fused with my bum flesh where I'd been sitting on them. They're still there now. Part of me forever.

I watched as two layers of my decaying skin just sloughed off on to the floor — like an old dead lizard.

Lovely.

Fancy dress parties? No thanks.

TWATLETS

These following stories are separate and small, but I think they belong here because they illustrate some lurking twatness without a doubt.

I am never unamazed (double negative – so what?) at the extent to which I'm prepared to delude myself if I need to. We all do this a bit, don't we? We know we shouldn't eat/drink/smoke/kill so much, but we want to, even if those things will take us to bad places, so we do. While we're actually engaged in the bad behaviours, we have an internal narrative that's quite different and persuasive, so we can permission-give ourselves, temporarily.

I am colossally skilled at this self-delusional stuff. I have plenty of ready-made excuses that serve my nefarious purposes, thank you.

Such as . . .

JESUS

Yes, I'm known to call upon my ol' chum to help out in moments of extreme stress. I think plenty of us, religious or not, do that when it serves our purpose. If there is a Jesus, I wonder if they are pissed off about this selective belief we exhibit . . . ? I would be.

Anyway, the time I mostly utilize my connection to the Lord (I have been a showbiz vicar after all, so I reckon I have a fast-track connection here) is when I board a plane. I don't really enjoy flying, but I pretend I do, so that I can get to places I need to be. I persuade myself that it's a perfectly humdrum thing to do — walk into a giant, heavy, metal tube and float about miles above solid ground. What on earth could go wrong?

My fake confidence goes some way to helping me fly . . . but I have a failsafe bit of twattery that I deploy pretty much every time and it ALWAYS works, because I haven't crashed to the ground in a hurtling torpedo of flaming fuselage YET. So that's solid hard proof enough for me.

I do this:

I decide that Jesus, the actual Jesus, who is, for the purpose of my needs, about a hundred and fifty foot tall, an actual giant no less, places his big, capable, beautiful alabaster hands around the actual plane I'm sitting in and lifts it – holds it throughout the flight – and gently places it down safely at wheresoever my particular destination is that day. I can go so far as to look out of the window of said plane and actually see his actual giant hands holding us actually up. During the flight, this is my certain reality. There is no other truth. It is fact. Actual fact.

Of course, all of the other passengers aboard also benefit from my preferential treatment. They temporarily become part of the elite, the blessed, the favoured. Like me. I allow this.

Thus far, this method has delivered me safely to every trip for about twenty years. Has any single one of those passengers on the same flight thanked me for the vicariously guaranteed safe passage? Not a single one. Unbelievable. It's only because of me THAT THEY ARE STILL ALIVE, and yet – nothing. Ingrates.

But, look – I'm beyond generous and I believe that it's right to spread the love, the safety, the privilege.

On top of the Jesus hands, I also provide the failsafe service of keeping the plane up with my knuckles. So long as I am clasping the arms of my seat so tight that the blood floods away from my knuckles leaving them taut and white, the plane seems to miraculously remain in the air.

Again, so far, no thanks whatsoever.

You're welcome.

ANAESTHETIC

I had to have a lil' procedure recently, which required me to go under anaesthetic.

I was all gowned up, on the gurney, just about to go into theatre, as were all the masked and rubber-gloved figures floating all around me, reassuring me that all would be well. The surgeon himself came to chivvy me on and I tried to make light of the whole scary situation by checking he wasn't drunk, had the correct spectacles on, etc., etc., ha ha ha. Lots of nervous laughs. They all humoured me, bless them.

The anaesthetist administered the miracle goo and, of course, the next thing I knew, I was waking up in the recovery room on the other side of theatre.

A nurse with the simple name badge 'Hope' was checking on me. Through the wooziness and as I resurfaced, I fixated on this name. I was suddenly horrendously emotional and over-grateful, so I started to babble on:

Me – Hello HOPE, and hello to HOPE generally, because that's what I had going into this and look, I'm here, so it worked. Just as I'd HOPED it would. Thank you so much for looking after me. I HOPE you don't mind. Honestly, thank you, I HOPE you know how much I appreciate all you do and all you are, and all you will be and have been. I love you, HOPE, and that's a fact, and I love all who know you and all who sail in you. I love your family and all your friends. Thank you, HOPE . . .

The surgeon turned up just as I was tipping into wholly unbearable.

Surgeon – All went well, no probs.

Me – Thank you. Thank you. Thank you. No, really, thank you for all you do, all you are . . .

Surgeon (interrupting the blether) – You certainly put me on my toes at the start!

Me – Thank you. Pardon? What? What do you mean?

Surgeon – You probably don't remember, but just as you were going under, you looked me right in the eyes and said:

Me – Don't kill me, I'm a National Treasure. No pressure.

Dear God, no. Please make it not true.

Luckily, he was laughing.

Me – I can't apologize enough. You see, my problem is that I'm a certified knob and major drugs will inevitably reveal that, won't they? I'm so sorry. Can I buy you anything to help you forgive me? A car or a house or something . . . ?

He was still laughing as he left me in the capable hands of poor Hope, who was also stifling a giggle.

Outed as a twat on the operating table.

Perfect.

TOFFEES

When the dreaded Covid came and stole our normal lives, there were various interesting challenges in our household. My husband runs a charity that helps folk who are in a pickle with alcohol or drugs or other tricky stuff, so he was classed as a front-line worker, meaning he still kept going to work. The health and safety advice he was given was that he had two options:

1. to move into accommodation near/at work

2. to come home, but take precautions, e.g. keep a distance from me and sleep in a separate room

We chose the latter. It was mighty strange. We didn't physically touch for quite a while and I found the separate sleeping properly upsetting. I decided somewhere along the line, I'm not sure when or how – it sort of crept up on me – to comfort myself in the loneliness of my empty-except-me bed with the succour of literal sucking.

Toffees.

Chocolate Eclair toffees to be precise.

And I was precise. Boy, was I.

It became ridiculously regimented.

It had to be five toffees, unwrapped and lined up on my bedside table.

Suck, suck, suck. Every night. Dementor-strength sucking.

This is AFTER BRUSHING MY TEETH!

I know. Appalling.

I'm sixty-five – what teeth I have are fragile and precious. What was I thinking?

Did I return to an infantile need for nursing myself somehow? Suckling on something sweet? Finding solace in sweets? Replacing husband with confectionery? (Not always a bad idea.)

Whatever the reason, the toffee habit became serious.

Other folk were ordering books and jigsaws online.

I was ordering toffees. In bulk.

I convinced myself it would stop the minute he returned to the bed. It was a good few weeks. The toffee dependence had its claws firmly into me.

He returned.

I had a choice – husband or toffees?

Or, if you have a kind husband – and I do – one who doesn't judge too quickly, there's no reason to give up either, surely?

This is when I had the grand epiphany.

Oh, I see.

I'm a GREEDY twat.

I want both.

So that's what happened.

Husband plus five toffees a night.

And that's where we still are, darlin' reader,

... nearly three years later.

Every night,

      five toffees.

Every day,

      thinner teeth. Less gum. More holes.

Yet another stunningly smart decision by French.

Not.

CONCORDE

Once upon a time, I was a vicar. Sorta.

Being that telly vicar brought some extraordinary opportunities to my doorstep.

One of them was genuinely surreal.

I have been asked many times to officiate at various weddings/ funerals/exorcisms and have politely declined, reminding the asker that I wasn't, in actuality, a real vicar. I find it odd that people can't differentiate between a genuine one and a pretend one who's just a twat in a dog collar, for shits 'n' giggles.

Anyhoo, a day came when I was asked if I would do the simple act of leading the grace at the start of a celebratory meal for an exceptional chap, who was retiring from a long career as senior cabin crew (purser?) at British Airways. Apparently, he was a fan of the show and his family and friends felt he would get a thrill if I turned up.

The fancy 'do' was being held in a hotel near my home outside Reading, so it was a no-brainer really. Plus, I was sent lots of info about this particular chap and it was clear he was something else.

An entire career full of charity and care on top of exemplary work, and he sounded like a hoot who definitely deserved all the treats he could have.

The dinner was due to be a surprise at the culmination of a day-long work conference, and the plan was that he would be led into the banquet hall blindfolded, the lights would be low and when they took the blindfold off, he would see all his family and chums, and me in full Geraldine Granger gear opposite him at a big central round table. I'd say grace and then say a quick hello to him and leave. Job done.

It didn't quite work out like that. I waited in a little bedroom, secreted away from the crowd while they finished their conference and prepared for the big dinner.

I clambered into all my vicar gear. Cassock, surplice, stole, dog-collar, chain with cross. I brushed my hair back behind my ears and looked in the mirror. There, staring back at me, was Geraldine, and I was suddenly overwhelmed with a gnawing discomfort. What I was doing was utterly fraudulent. In fact, I think it might've even been illegal. I don't think you're allowed to impersonate a person of the cloth. Of course, I already had done, many times, but it was when cameras were there, when there was a script and a TV show.

This was sort of real.

Not REALLY real.

But still, a bit dodgy.

And I was about to say grace.

Anyone CAN say grace, that ain't illegal.

But not dressed like this, surely . . . ?

I started to get icy feet, but it was way too late to back out now. I'd be letting everyone down.

They came to collect me and I walked through the hushed crowd to my place opposite the man, who still had his blindfold on.

Oh heck.

Blindfold off, lights up, HUGE CHEER!

Blinking, the man looks at me in utter disbelief and he opens his mouth and, no word of a lie, he screams at the top of his lungs for a full five minutes non-stop. He is fantastically camp and his screeching knows no ceiling when it comes to top notes. Eardrums are sacrificed for his pleasure.

I am unable to start the grace until he eventually calms down.

I'm still worrying about the moral propriety of what I'm doing. Why? It's ludicrous.

So, I decide to mash up the grace, which is, frankly, probably a worse offence.

Me – Dearly Beloveds and also sneaky bitches, we are gathered here to celebrate (insert name – I won't), so let us give thanks for this delicious meal and . . . say GRACE.

I wait. Room is silent.

Me (shouting) – I said, SAY GRACE!

Whole room repeats – Grace.

Me – Thank you, and in the words our Lord taught us: yum, yum in my tum, tomorrow morning out my bum. Bless You. Amen.

I kiss the man, who is screaming again. I talk to his darlin's; I eat supper (free food, I'm not leaving early); I watch the slide show all about him and listen to the glorious speeches and then I head home.

The payment for this job was a return flight to New York on Concorde.

WOW!

I was so excited, but so nervous. It goes even faster than normal planes, so I'd REALLY need Jesus's hands for this one, but I feared that Jesus might not come out to play this time since I'd diddled about with the grace. So, I made the fantastically sound decision to get immediately bladdered instead, so I'd be spark out when we fell out of the sky as punishment. I had four Camparis.

This meant I immediately fell asleep, missing all the Mach/speed fun and all the freebies and food that I was so looking forward to.

When I woke up, I was FULLY leaning on the poor man next to me, with my head on his shoulder as if I were his baby daughter or perhaps more like his old, dying dog. As I snorted awake, I notice I'd dribbled all down his expensive suit. Red Campari dribble.

He saw it. I saw it. Neither of us spoke of it.

So, there we have it – travel twat, extraordinaire.

THEATRE

DUSTIN HOFFMAN

I love doing theatre work. I seem to do it less as I get older and am more reluctant to leave home in Cornwall, but some of my most favourite work memories are from theatre.

I once worked out that I'd done eight plays or something like that, and each of them was roughly a six-month theatre run, so I've spent four solid years of my life onstage every day, and that's without tours or panto. Believe me, this is NOTHING compared to real theatre creatures like Simon Russell Beale or Judi Dench or Mark Rylance whose theatre tally must run into decades. Without doubt, it's a bug, and if you catch it, you're in for life one way or another, and it's futile to resist.

So, some of the most extraordinary and extreme forms of twatting I've been part of in my life happen when there's a group of twats – or 'celebrities' as we're sometimes referred to . . .

CELEBRITWATS, if you will.

What is the correct collective noun for us, I wonder? Maybe 'a repugnance of twats' is most apt?

Anyhoo – such a group was assembled one evening in my dressing room after a performance of a play called *Me and Mamie O'Rourke*, a show I did in the West End with Fatty Saunders. It was written by Mary Agnes Donoghue, the screenwriter of the wonderful film *Beaches* with Bette Midler starring. She's American, the director of the play Bob Ackerman is American. Somehow back then, being American seemed fantastically glamorous.

On this particular evening, there was a group of celebritwats in attendance, including my good friend Richard Curtis, who wrote *The Vicar of Dibley*, along with some friends of his. The first Mr French was there, a bloke called Lenny Henry, with some of his chums, and there were also a couple of non-celebs who aren't in showbusiness, known to us as 'muggles'.

Bit rude.

Joke.

There was a buzz that night because of who was on the guest list, in the audience to watch the play. Twiggy and her husband Leigh Lawson were in and they'd brought their great chum, Hollywood star Dustin Hoffman.

DUSTIN HOFFMAN, FOR DOGS' SAKE!!

Him off *Midnight Cowboy* and *The Graduate* and *Kramer vs Kramer* and *Tootsie* and on and on. A proper grown-up big posh actor.

From America. Fantastically glamorous.

We were beside, above, beneath and inside ourselves with excitement, as we waited patiently, all crammed together in my small dressing room. I kept my blonde wig on and my big fake eyelashes in the pathetic hope of impressing Hollywood star Dustin Hoffman. It's impossible to take off a wig and the stocking-cap beneath plus a faceful of big make-up and look presentable in the five minutes it takes for the audience to get round to the stage door and into the dressing room. You are left looking like an undercooked bap with a scrubbed face and silly, just-pinned-up-sweaty-straggle-hair. Not a great look to meet Hollywood star Dustin Hoffman.

Eventually, there's a little rap on the door and the crowded room goes quiet as we crane our necks to see who's coming in. First in is Twiggy, followed by Leigh. There is a lot of squealing from us all as we hug each other, and actor-y greetings are exchanged.

Then there is the moment.

We are all watching the door.

The anticipation is vulva-level high.

Is he coming?

Perhaps he won't?

But – Hollywood star Dustin Hoffman is an experienced actor of some substance. He knows how to make an entrance. You keep the audience waiting . . .

Finally, after what felt like five years, he comes around the door. Hollywood star Dustin Hoffman is in the room, ladies and gentlemen. No doubt.

He plants himself firmly with legs apart, confident as all hell. He locks eyes with only me. Thrilling. He points at me (rude) and what happens next is genuinely one of the most bizarre experiences of my life. He is marking me with his very purposeful point, and he starts to advance towards me. I'm sitting, he is moving towards me, bearing down on me, repeating the same word over and over again . . . ooo . . . about thirty times,

Hollywood star Dustin Hoffman – Actress! Actress! Actress! Actress! Actress.

Frankly, I did not know what to do with my face. Or anything. But especially my face.

I smiled initially, then as the volley of repetitions came at me thick 'n' fast, I transitioned into nervous giggling and on into full-on gurning.

He did one last affirmative point accompanied by a resolute 'Actress!' right in my face.

All I could think of to respond was 'Nkyou' in a rather feeble sycophantic voice.

He fixed me with one bizarre last stare, then moved on to acknowledge the others in the room. He's polite in that way, gotta give him that. He shook hands with everyone, and when he reached Richard it went like this:

Hollywood star Dustin Hoffman – What are you up to?

Richard – Well, I'm actually writing the second series of a sitcom I do with Dawn, it's called *The Vicar of Dibley* and she plays a female priest.

Small pause, then . . . astonishingly

Hollywood star Dustin Hoffman – She plays a priest? I'll direct that. Call me.

Ummmmmmmmmm . . .

WHAAAAAT?!?!

What is he talking about?

Hollywood star Dustin Hoffman wants to direct *The Vicar of Dibley*?

EH? Can you imagine? I mean – lovely and flattering and all that, but . . . really?

Is he mad?

Whassamatterhim?

Bonkers.

But of course, I'm smiling away like an unctuously grateful greasy git.

I remind you, I have no idea what to do with my face. I don't have any expressions that fit this absurd moment. I only have my go-to idling idiot expression available, so I deploy that to its fullest effect.

It's genuinely hideous.

I'm giving raw undiluted fucknuckle twat.

Hollywood star Dustin Hoffman continues along the line of people, greeting everyone individually. He is getting closer and closer to Lenny. I can clearly see that Len is panicking. HSDH is one of his acting heroes. He is far too over-excited to meet him and already the last few minutes are jam-packed with weird . . .

There are two important things you should know at this point, darlin' reader:

1. Len is the KING of faux pas – to a catastrophic degree. There are many examples too numerous and cruel to mention but, as a quick e.g., he once asked my friend how her dad was, on the evening of said dad's funeral, when she was coming to ours for a comforting supper . . . y'know, stuff like that . . .

2. Hollywood star Dustin Hoffman is not tall. Suffice to say, he sleeps in a matchbox.

Len is, of course, the opposite. He's a whole depth high, about 6'3" or so at his proudest upright.

So – tall is meeting short.

Hollywood star Dustin Hoffman is moving closer, closer. LH is getting more and more fidgety.

He's swaying a bit.

A sure sign he's readying himself.

Eventually, Hollywood star and hero of Len is standing right opposite him.

Len looks down at him, and as they shake hands, a moment LH could only have dreamt of, LH utters the immortal and regrettable words:

Len – HI, BIG GUY!

OK.

It's happened.

Those words are in the public domain. They've been literally said. Out loud.

Time stops.

The air is thick with fat cringe.

I eat my chair with my actual bum hole.

Uber-clench.

Hollywood star Dustin Hoffman swiftly moves on. Wise. He is adjacent to the door and he knows it's time to leave, but of course, he's not going without a final flourish, is he? No.

He turns at the door, locks eyes with me once more, and starts the pointing gesture . . .

Oh Lord, we're off again.

This time, the repeated word is different.

I've been promoted, as he repeats,

Hollywood star Dustin Hoffman – Artist. Artist. Artist. Artist x thirty times.

And he's gone.

For some reason I will never fully understand, call it relief, I jump up and immediately start to applaud him loudly.

Me – Hollywood star Dustin Hoffman, ladies and gentlemen!

As if he was leaving the stage after a play. Which he sort of was.

Three major twats in that story. Me. Len. Hollywood star Dustin Hoffman.

MARVELLOUS WORK.

CURTAIN CALL

Staying in the theatre, here's a story illustrating a particularly twatty moment I had.

It was 2003, and I was in a one-woman play called *My Brilliant Divorce* written by Irish writer Geraldine Aron.

The experience of being on stage on my own was mighty odd for me. I hadn't toured any of my own shows at this point, so I'd thus far been on stage with either Fatty or with a whole cast in a play. It's only when you are on your own that you come to realize that a huge, wonderful part of doing this job is working alongside other folk you enjoy being around. Every play is a new microcosm of a family, albeit temporary. As for Fatty . . . well, that's me at my most comfortable, collaborating and mainly laughing with my comedy sister.

So, if we're honest, the reason to do theatre is to be with a gang, and:

Have people to go out for dinner with

Have people to give first-night presents to

Have people to share nerves with

Have people to share in-jokes with

Have people to criticize the director with

Have people to be annoyed by

Have people to flirt with

Have people to regret flirting with

Have people to moan with

Because quite honestly, that is what actors do best when all together – moan. We are BRILLIANT at it. Whingeing and nosey-parkering are our favourite pastimes. We have skills.

Anyhoo, there I was, all on my tod at the Apollo Theatre on Shaftesbury Avenue, doin' my facin' the front and showin' off every night.

Two doors up at the Lyric Theatre, was a very serious play by Strindberg called *The Dance of Death*, which is every bit as cheerful as its title suggests.

It's a Dance. Of. Death.

You know that sort of play that is heavy, with lots of subtext and metaphor that requires us the audience to pretend to understand? (That might just be me.) It's a substantial play that requires proper acting chops, and the three main actors in it certainly have those.

Ian McKellen, Frances de la Tour and Owen Teale. I'm lucky enough to know Ian and Owen quite well and I'd certainly met Frances because her brother Andy was a regular on the alternative comedy circuit with us guys in the eighties.

They had their matinees on the same day of the week as me – Wednesday – but their play was longer than mine. On this particular Wednesday, I came offstage after my curtain call and I immediately felt a bit sad that yet again, I was on my own backstage, so I decided to spontaneously pay them a visit.

I took off my stage costume and put on my jeans and trainers and my baggy hoodie and I pelted round to the stage door of their theatre. I'd been in and out to see them a bit, so the stage door keeper let me through straight away, no question.

There's a very particular hush backstage in a theatre when a play is in progress. It's like being in church. People creep about ninja-quietly and only speak in hushed tones. The play is EVERYTHING and is respected. The hallowed contract between audience and performer is in process. Nothing could interrupt that. The actors and crew have spent hours creating a world, a suspension of disbelief, an alternative reality. It would be awful to ruin it. Disrespectful. So, I stood quietly in the wings at the side of the stage watching the last few crucial minutes of the play. The denouement, where the playwright wraps it all up skilfully. I had joked in the past few weeks that I wished I was in the cast alongside them all. In his cups one night, Ian bestowed upon me the part of Maria, the maid who is heard to slam a door offstage as she is storming off, somewhere near the beginning of the play. The character never appears on stage so I was awarded this part in an honorary way as a bit of a gag. A lovely, inclusive gag.

The play finished. The audience burst into applause, and the actors lined up for the curtain call, a carefully rehearsed order of bows. I watched from the wings as they all took their moment, bathed in light and approval.

It was a lovely sight.

Here came Frances de la Tour – audience loved her.

Here came Owen Teale – audience loved him.

Here came magnificent Ian McKellen (known to me as 'Serena': Sir – Ian – a). The audience ADORED him.

The three lead actors beckoned the other, supporting actors on to the stage from the wings.

Standing near me was a lovely woman who played a member of the house-staff, I think, and as she started to move on stage, and in a moment of spontaneous and staggering audacity, I took her hand and went into the light on stage next to her.

There I was, in the line-up.

Taking a bow for a play I wasn't in.

This must have been somewhat confusing for the audience. The play is set in Sweden in the 1900s.

I was not.

I was set in London in my trainers in 2003.

Never mind.

I was loving it.

Lapping it up. Bow. Bow. Bow. Thank you. Yes.

Especially loving that the lead actors in the centre of the line had absolutely NO IDEA I was there.

Why did I do it? Probably mainly, if I'm honest, for the cheek and the thrill and the funnies.

Yes, but also I'm a needy show-off, and in that bizarre choice, I exposed some true feelings of wanting to belong in a gang, wanting to be part of something, rather than being alone.

But mainly because ... I'm a supreme twat.

Serena had his revenge when he turned up at my final curtain call in full character soldier costume and presented me with a salute and a bouquet of cabbages ...

SPAGHETTI SKETCH

Many years ago, I took part in a Revue called *Then Again* at the Lyric Theatre in Hammersmith, directed by the extraordinary Neil Bartlett. He'd assembled four of us la-di-das to perform sketches together. Sheila Hancock, Des Barrit, Neil Mullarkey and yours truly.

Neil had collated a selection of sketches from various different eras and we started rehearsals. As with all revue/sketch formats, some sketches were more successful than others, for a variety of reasons, and we gradually started to cull any we didn't think were working. We were suddenly a bit short on content, so there was a crisis meeting about who to contact to write more, or whether there were other sketches or songs that already existed which we could consider. Before long, there were tried and tested Harold Pinter and Richard Curtis sketches on the table for consideration along with others, and I for one felt confident that we were creeping towards a more solid show. It was a seat of the pants experience, pretty volatile, while the five of us often disagreed about what was funny and what wasn't.

It was a situation where all of us had to come out of our comfort zones in one way or another. I, for instance, felt particularly awkward with the songs and little dance routines we did to top and tail the show. I'd never done anything like this EXCEPT to take the piss out of it, so I found it absurd. Sheila was an anchor for me because she'd done revues before with the likes of the brilliant Beryl Reid, etc., so I trusted her taste. Plus, she's Sheila bloody Hancock and she's fantastic. The four of us were very different, so finding common ground wasn't easy; it was a challenging exercise in compromise and support.

I started to feel the nip of fear and to my shame, I retreated into my own corner a bit. Although I took part in other sketches, I felt less confident about those, and less willing to experiment as the opening night loomed and I felt panic set in. I wanted to make decisions and stick to them to give us all a chance to learn what we had. I wasn't alone in my anxiety, it was obvious with all four of us, so the day came when we had a pretty robust conversation with Neil. That means a little mutiny. It wasn't nice, but it felt necessary.

During the rather fractious discussion, Sheila suggested doing a sketch she knew of, which she felt was a sure-fire winner. It was a slapstick routine, involving a couple eating spaghetti in an Italian restaurant. It offered parts for all four of us, so we had an initial bash at it and I instantly disliked it; I found it too silly, too broad, too messy and not funny enough. I didn't warm to the buffoonery and I couldn't see how it could work unless it was performed by clowns in a circus. I was stood down from this sketch and left the three of them to it. I didn't wish it ill, but I was certain it wouldn't work. CERTAIN.

THAT SKETCH brought the house down EVERY NIGHT. I would watch in bewildered awe from the wings, as the gales of laughter rolled in from the audience who were helpless with joyful guffawing. It was a slam dunk winner at every performance, and where was I?

Off stage wondering how I could've got it so badly wrong.

I totally misjudged it.

What a huge lesson in humility that was. I had to accept that I have copious blind spots, and it's good to recognize them when I get the chance, otherwise repeating the same ruddy mistake is a big likelihood.

Just watch me. I'm sure to misjudge stuff over and over – BUT – maybe less often as I learn a bit more?

Maybe.

Then again – I am a twat, so . . .

Maybe not.

SPEAKIE DIALOGUE IN OTHER LANGUAGES AND ACCENTS

OPERA

Imagine this.

It was 2006, and my agent Maureen Vincent received a call from the Royal Opera House, checking my availability and willingness to be in an opera by Donizetti called *La Fille du Régiment*, directed by a renegade young French director, Laurent Pelly. When she called to tell me this, I had a good five minutes of living in a deluded parallel universe before she explained further.

Inside my head during those five minutes:

'At last, SOMEONE has finally recognized that at the heart and core of me, I'm really a singer. Not JUST a singer, but a vocal phenomenon, as yet unknown to most. In fact, ONLY known to me, in my car, in my shower, in my . . . mind. How in the helling hell does that young buck of a foreign director know this about me? Has he happened to walk past my open bathroom window when I'm in full voice, perchance? Is that how he has witnessed my virtuoso expertise? My remarkable coloratura? The wonder that is vocal me? The whole, entire magnificence of me and my astounding pipes? (Upper pipes, that is, not lower pipes — which are also marvellous, but that's a whole other book.) Yes, yes, yes, I must accept this job and allow the opera world in on the revelation, let the world receive me in all my diva glory. Here I come, La Scala, the Met . . . but first, the Royal Opera House . . . tra la la.'

♪♫♪♪ ♪♫♪♪

Maureen abruptly interrupts my idiotic reverie, and quickly disabuses me of any deluded operatic dreams.

Maureen – No, love, love, love. Listen. This is a speaking part. Only. Just talkie. No singee. I suspect they'll get the professionals in for that . . .

Rude.

Oh. Right. So I'm going to be on stage at the actual Royal Opera House, but I'm not going to sing a single cocking note.

I see. Disappointing. Their loss.

Rehearsals began, and boy did I quickly realize that opera and theatre are two entirely different beasts.

I was very excited to hear the voices of our two leads, Juan Diego Flórez, the Peruvian tenor, and Natalie Dessay, the French soprano. I'd been told by opera chums that these two especially were remarkable and that I was in for an ear treat. On the very first day they both entered the rehearsals, I was fully charged with anticipation. Here we go, prepare to have yer head blown off with giant exquisite sound . . .

But no.

Opera singers don't sing out properly in rehearsals; they use tiny voices while they're working it all out. I didn't know this, so I was quietly thinking, 'No, mates, this little soft singing ain't gonna cut it with a British audience, I'm tellin' you right now. Opera tickets are a bleedin' fortune, they're gonna want you to belt it.'

Thankfully, before I could actually deliver this sage advice, someone explained it to me. Opera singers understandably preserve their voices, until the dress run when, let me assure you, your skull explodes with the exhilarating force of it all.

Anyway, anyway, anyway, my character was called the Duchess of Krakenthorp, and she's a gorgon. She's cruel to the young heroine of the piece. A proper baddie and good fun to play.

In the rehearsal room, many many languages were being spoken. There were Spanish and Italian and French voices, and everyone seemed to be fluent in everyone else's language.

Except me, of course.

I'm barely fluent in the English wot I speakie every day.

This part required me to speak in formal French.

Right. OK. Yes, it's a challenge, but let's consider a couple of key points:

1. I did French 'O' level. All right, I only got an E, but it's still a pass. Just.

2. I had a French penpal called Odette once, and I wrote some French words to her in a letter. Also once. (Then she came and stayed with me and stole my boyfriend because being French meant that her mouth was in a permanent state of pout-kiss that he apparently was helpless to resist.)

3. I'm called Dawn FRENCH, excuse me. I'm likely of Huguenot descent, so I've got a little bit of garlic in ze blood, non? I'm virtually French. Actual French.

So – in rehearsals, I was giving it my best haw-he-haw French words and accent, and I was hearing myself and feeling quietly confident. Yep. I was sounding proper French. Like a French person. Like I was born there. Like I'm French.

Then...

One day, quite early on in the rehearsals, Laurent the director and his French assistant Agathe, took me aside for a little chat.

Agathe translated for Laurent, who spoke very little English. It started well,

Agathe – Laurent sez he like very much what you are doing. It is very funny and very courageous because it is so bad. Zis bad French we call Franglais. Nobody is speaking zis bad French on zis stage for hundred years. He zink you are very, how you say – brave. Continue like zat.

I was gutted, thought I'd been pulling it off, but of course, I gave Laurent the thumbs up, as if to say 'Great. My bad French plan is working well.' I was giving him my giant demented wolf smile simultaneously.

That was MY VERY BEST FRENCH.

They thought it was a joke.

Thanks a lot, Lawrence and Agatha – which is what your names really are in proper English. Not that sexy, actually.

So glad I could provide you with a big ol' belly laugh at my ineptitude with accents.

I made sure I had the last laugh though.

I didn't want to leave that hallowed hall without singing a note. How could I boast to folk that I'd sung on stage at the Royal Opera House if I HADN'T?! So, on the very last night, as the Duchess of Krakenthorp was leaving the stage in my final exit, I turned round and sang one long (probably quite tuneless) note to accompany the word 'Merde'.

Then I swept off. Twat.

NUNS

Maybe not surprisingly, it turns out that I'm quite twatty all round with accents. I can do a passable West Country accent because that's where I'm from.

There was one occasion when Fatty Saunders and I wrote a sketch where we played novice nuns, who were on a convent outing to the Vatican, in the hope of seeing their absolute crush, the Pope.

Of course, they spent most of their time in the souvenir shop buying stupid stuff like pillows with his face on that they could snog. Obviously, this sketch required Irish accents.

Jennifer gave her best Amanda Burton impression, which means she was hovering somewhere north of the border. I chose to do a version of a children's Saturday morning TV light entertainment, leprechaun puppet-type of accent.

Sort of patronizing.

Borderline offensive.

No, actually . . . just offensive.

When it aired, I knew how bad it was, because I received a call from my chum Kathy Burke, who is of Irish descent, and she said,

Kathy – If you ever attempt another Irish accent, I will end you.

So – message received loud and clear.

I have a Gaelic fatwa on me.

Lovely.

Listen, I'm not scared of Kathy bleddy Burke.

'Top o' th'mornin' to ye, Kathy Burke, and B'Jaysus.'

Actually – I am a bit scared of Kathy Burke ...

Don't tell her I said that, OK? Promise now.

Shhhhhhhhhhhhhhhhhhhh!

THE NILE

Yet another shining example of my epic failing when it comes to accents is when Sir Kenneth of the Branagh invited Fatty and me to be in his giant Hollywood blockbusting Agatha Christie thriller, *Death on The Nile*.

This was knicker-wettingly exciting, and quite a bold move by the Kenneth, to put the pair of us alongside each other in a big flick like this, considering the fact that whenever we are together in a film, it's usually to take the mick. Nevertheless, he asked and we willingly obliged.

Ken was to play Poirot, reprising his role from the previous film, *Murder on the Orient Express*. He was also to direct, produce and be involved with the writing. This was a MASSIVE commitment for him, and one he took very seriously. He is a strict taskmaster, but he's also the most hospitable director for an actor to work with. Plus, he has the spirit of very naughty indeed propelling him on.

Anyhoo, he invited us to a meeting to discuss our characters. He wanted us to bed them in properly, pin them down authentically.

The two characters we were playing, Marie Van Schuyler, a communist, and Bowers, her nurse companion, were American. We'd been sent the script weeks before and it was quickly evident that Ken was labouring under the misconception that we might have thought about it and done some preparation.

Preposterous idea.

We'd been VERY BUSY ... umm ... y'know ... eating biscuits and thinking about *The Real Housewives of New Jersey*. Far too busy to put in the minutes required to lay the groundwork for a successful performance, thank you.

We went to the meeting and he was quite intense about the research he imagined we'd surely done ...

Ken – So Dawn, your character, Bowers, what is she reading at the moment?

I am utterly poleaxed.

I can't remember the name of a single book ever written, never mind a book from the correct period ...

Me – Umm, she is reading . . . a book. Or a magazine. Or a comic. I think.

He looks blankly at me.

Ken – OK, so who does she mix with? Who does she know . . . ?

Me – Um . . . people?

Ken – Right. What did she eat for breakfast?

Me – Um . . . toast?

He stares at me. I can't fool him. I give it one further pathetic stab . . .

Me – Coco Pops?

I know zero, nothing, nada. It is patently clear that we are massively ill-prepared. Not an auspicious start.

He is kind. He doesn't kill us. He sends us off to steep ourselves in the characters, to saturate ourselves, to RESEARCH. It's not a lot to ask. It's what actors are supposed to do. It's the least actors should do.

So we do.

We go home and do our homework. Finally.

Yes, these characters are American, through and through.

CUT TO:

The readthrough a few weeks later.

A readthrough is a daunting old thing because this is the first time you meet all the other actors, plus the top knobs from the studios, etc. are also in attendance.

The readthrough takes place in Egypt.

I know, right?

I bet you think Egypt is in Egypt.

Well, it isn't. It's in the M3 corridor near Cobham in a place called Longcross Studios, where Ken has miraculously re-created the temples at Karnak, the Nile, Pyramids, markets and an entire thirties steam paddler. The whole spectacle of the set is astonishing and on top of ALL the wonder – it's only five minutes from Ken's house.

How lucky is that?!

Back to the readthrough – Fatty and I are sitting next to each other around a vast table with all the others, and there are many different accents in the room.

Gal Gadot is Israeli playing American

Rose Leslie is a Scot playing French

Ken is from Reading playing Belgian

Ali Fazal is Indian playing American

Annette Bening is American playing English

Tom Bateman is English playing English

Russell Brand is Essex playing British

Sophie Okonedo is London playing Deep South

Letitia Wright is Brit/Guyanese playing Deep South

and on and on, with many others . . .

The readthrough starts and Jennifer is the first of us two to speak and she sounds authentically American. Well done, Fatty.

Then it's my go.

I start and . . . yes . . . yes actually . . . yes, it sounds quite good, and I allow myself to lean into it wholeheartedly, twanging away like an American local. Yep, darn it, we're going to pull this off. In fact, I'm ever so slightly impressed with us. Bravo, the French and the Saunders.

We finish the readthrough. It's genuinely fantastic and there's a round of applause from all. Hurray. We exchange encouraging pleasantries, then Fatty and I head home. The filming is due to start a couple of days later.

I've been home only a couple of minutes before the call comes from one of the producers:

Important producer – Dawn, hi. We've had a little rethink.

Ah, OK, I think, I've been sacked. They want Lumley. Yep, this has happened to me before.

Important producer continues – We're thinking you should be British.

Oh, I see. I'm not sacked, I'm just shit at the accent.

Me – Right, yes, right, OK, yes, fine, yes. I agree, yes, good decision, right, yes, fine. (I'm babbling my cringey acquiescence.) Umm . . . what about Jennifer? Is she . . . ?

I pause and wait to hear their decision . . .

Important producer – She's still American.

Me – Yep, good. She's American because . . . well, because she's good at it, sounds . . . American, I expect? Umm, absolutely fine. I get it. No prob. Just one little thing . . . what about all the big backstory, y'know, all the research I did . . . to . . . y'know . . . bed in the character . . . of . . . Miss Bowers?

Important producer – Bin it.

Me – Bin it. Right. Yep. Will do. Bye.

So I binned it, turned up on the Monday, and did the facing front and showing off, with an English accent. Same costume, different accent.

How entirely cringey was all that?

This was a nail in the coffin of my surety that I really mustn't take on parts that require big accents. I didn't properly know this about myself until this particular job, but it doesn't hurt (it does, but it doesn't ultimately matter) to be gently guided towards something you should understand about yourself. Acknowledging the edges of your talent is really OK.

In fact, what's not OK is to battle on when it's clear to all about you that you're clinging to the wreckage of a sliver of a skill that is, frankly, not going to support you. It's best to operate well inside your skillset, and for me that's NOT great big accents.

I once read the fantastic Neil Gaiman's dark fantasy novella Coraline *for an audiobook recording. Jennifer and I played two of the characters, Miss Forcible and Miss Spink, in the animated version, but this was me in an audio studio for several days, reading it aloud and giving all the characters a voice. There are children, adults, cats and all manner of strangeness and wonder in this phenomenal book. I loved doing it, trying to find subtle changes for each different character.*

SIDEBAR

Only an uber TWAT would get to the end of three days' worth of recording without realizing that a major character called Mr Bobinksy is, of course, Polish. Any attempt at something even vaguely Eastern European might have helped, but a man called MR BOBINSKY...! I simply did a deep voice. To indicate 'man'. Duh.

Honestly?

Dear God.

Confirmed twatting right there.

The engineer in the gallery was a bit shocked:

Engineer – Oh dear, do you want to start again?

Me – No, ta. It'll be fine.

Then I ran away very fast.

CRUSH TWAT

I have a badly behaved much-loved West-Ham-supporting friend who just happens to be a staggeringly good writer, called Tony Grounds. He wrote a one-off telly drama called *Sex and Chocolate* for me in 1997. He's canny, he knows I'm going to say yes to ANYTHING with that title, aren't I? It was a touching story about infidelity and the damage it wreaks. We needed to cast a two-tone-loving husband. I was absolutely delighted when Phil Daniels, an actor I'd long admired, accepted the part.

How fantastic is he in pretty much everything he's ever been in? *Quadrophenia*? *Scum*? Working on 'Parklife' with Blur? I was such a fan. Still am. Truth be told, I was in awe of him, and consequently equally excited and anxious about working with him. It would've broken my heart to not get on with him, but of course I knew absolutely nothing about him in real life. I knew who did. M'chum Kathy Burke. So, I called her and asked what he was like.

Kath – Aww, he's diamond.

Me – Oh good. Phew.

Kath – . . . IF he likes you . . . he don't suffer wankers.

Right. Ah, that might be a problem. I'm 100 per cent wanker. Confirmed.

That was it then. I decided to put on a personality fireworks display just for him. Watch me sparkle!

First Red Twat Flag

Rehearsals began, and the lovely kind director Gavin Millar suggested that we improvise a bit because he wanted us to interact like a real family before the cameras started rolling. Phil was the husband, and we had a couple of teenage kids in the story, so Gavin encouraged us to hang out together on a mocked-up set, to cook and eat and dance and be an authentic family. In amongst all the improvising he urged us to be physically easy together. Y'know, BE a loving husband and wife, have a little smooch, be less inhibited, touch each other as you would. A little kiss here and there. A brush past each other as you stand at the cooker. Normal stuff. Natural.

It was a little bit awkward to begin with, but we soon eased into it, and there were lots of laughs.

This was called 'work', apparently.

It was utterly thrilling and I was bleddy LOVING it.

I was loving it too much.

FAR TOO MUCH!

So – filming started, and quite early on in the schedule, we had some quite intimate bed scenes to be shot over two days. Nothing pervy, but plenty of snuggling, kissing and some serious dialogue about the marriage and the threat to it.

On the morning of the first day of these scenes, this is how my morning went:

Wake up at home in bed with my husband Len.

Have a cuddle with him.

Get out of bed.

Get undressed.

Get in shower.

Get dressed.

Go to work.

Get undressed.

Get into bed with Phil Daniels.

I know. Unusual.

Filming scenes like these is very strange. In one way, it's not intimate at all because so many people are fussing and faffing all around you. Ordinary film-set conversations are going on, about lighting or camera positions, and a make-up artist is primping you, so it's all quite public and therefore rendered ordinary.

But.

In another way, it IS intimate because it's still skin on skin, lips on lips. It's still exchanging breath with someone you've come to quite like.

So.

Whilst we were doing these scenes, I started to get giddy. All the signals were mixed. Ordinarily, if you are witnessed snogging someone who isn't your husband, the folk around you should be disapproving and quickly hold you to account. Instead, on a film set, you receive applause, approval and a request to do it again.

And.

I was thinking – 'Yes, let's do it again.'

Third Red Twat Flag

When the end of this first day of intimate scenes came, this is how my evening went:

I climbed out of bed with my telly husband Phil Daniels.

I got dressed.

I went home.

I got undressed.

I got into bed with my actual husband.

I waited for him to fall asleep and I sat up in the bed and stayed up like that all night fretting, my mind spinning like a thousand fiery Catherine wheels on bonfire night.

I felt like a total shit.

Because.

Now, I was entirely in love with Phil Daniels.

AAAAARGH!

What was going to happen?

Everything was about to change.

My whole life was going to be tipped up, because Phil Daniels and I were going to be together forever. We couldn't possibly deny this giant love we had, it was too mighty.

I would have to exit this marriage.

I would have to sell this house I loved.

I would have to find a new house with Phil – I didn't even know where he wanted to live . . . ?

What was going to happen with the custody of my little daughter?

OH. MY. GOD.

After five million hours of night:

I get out of bed without hugging my husband because I am now a certified adulteress whore.

I get undressed.

I shower.

I get dressed.

I go to work.

I get undressed.

I get back into bed with my new darling, Phil.

At last.

I've been away from him for too long. What's it been? Ten hours or something – unbearable when the love is so new and so very potent. I practically DIED of separation sorrow in that awful dark time without him.

Sliding back into bed next to him is bliss, but I'm nervous, bursting with this gigantic irrefutable love and the certainty that Phil Daniels and I are going to be one. For always.

I'm also anxious because I know that the minute I tell Phil, EVERYTHING is going to change. FOREVER. Our whole lives will be different. This is a seismic shift for us both.

Halfway through the morning, there's a tea break and everyone disappears for a brew, but Phil and I, we stay in the bed because ... y'know ... we're comfortable there.

This is it.

I know I must seize the moment.

I lean in towards him, and he simultaneously leans in towards me and whispers in my ear,

Phil – Can I tell you something?

Me (in my head) – Yes, my darling, you can. We both know what you're going to say, we must follow our hearts, we are slaves to love.

Me (out loud) – Yes, of course.

Phil – See that bird over there? (He's pointing at the pretty young costume assistant.)

Me – Yes?

Phil – Tell you what, if I wasn't happily married, I'd let her see the inside of my Winnebago. She's beautiful, ain't she?

EXCUSE ME, BUT PARDON THE ACTUAL FUCK?!

He smashes my heart into billions of shattered shards in one fell strike. It is instant and brutal.

Me – Yes, she is certainly very lovely. Indeed.

It turns out Phil Daniels had NO IDEA we were totally in love. He had not a clue that I was about to sacrifice everything in my life for him and only him. He was ignorant of the fact that he was my forever person.

I was devastated.

But.

What happened in the very next instant was very interesting.

In the microsecond between the rejection and the realization, in that sliver between the two moments – I fell OUT OF LOVE with Phil Daniels and I chucked him.

NEVER MEET YOUR IDOLS

My love for David Cassidy was physically painful. Parts of me genuinely hurt when I thought about him. It could have been conflated with the normal growing pains of a thirteen- to eighteen-year-old girl, but I don't think so. No one would know how to love David the way I would. All the others were fools and silly smitten teenagers, whereas I was totally grounded, sensible and serious about my devotion. I wrote letters explaining to him that he could find sanctuary in my home, that we would feed him nutritious food and I would endeavour to look after his mental and especially PHYSICAL well-being. I even promised to ALWAYS tell him the 'honest truth', unlike all the 'yes-men' I presumed must surround him in the heady world of showbusiness and music. Yes, I was pledging to pretty much manage his career if he so chose.

I wrote poems to him. Some of the lines MIGHT have been directly plagiarized from Dylan Thomas . . . or Holly Hobbie . . . but hey. When the naked photo of him by Annie Leibovitz on the front cover of *Rolling Stone* started circulating, I actually felt annoyed that he was revealing himself to others, an intimacy that should rightly have been preserved for me, surely? I was definitely peeved, but I was also massively aroused and insane with desire for David-belongs-to-me-and-me-only-Cassidy. It hurts to be a teenager consumed with an infatuation so intoxicating it actually renders you breathless and sobbing hormone-heavy tears on a regular, inexplicable basis. You are alone with your pain. Absolutely no one understands it, especially not your family who use words like 'silly' when you try to explain your devotion. On one occasion my own brother described me as 'a soppy eejit', as he thrust the sword of ridicule directly into my poor hurting heart.

All it would've taken to make me blissfully happy, would've been for David to reach out, even just once. Just a word. Just a gesture. Just ... please ... please ... PLEEEEEEEEEEEEEEEEEEEEEEEEEEEE EEEEEEEEEEEEEEEEEEEEAASE!

But – nothing. I was bereft.

CUT TO:

About thirty years later. Maureen, my agent, calls me one day out of the blue to say that David Cassidy's 'people' have been in touch. They know via my autobiography, that I had a tremendous crush on him in my teens.

He is appearing in London, at the Hammersmith Apollo, I think it was.

Apparently, David would like to invite me to appear alongside him onstage. I would be required to sit on a chair onstage whilst he would sing 'Cherish' to me.

To ME. And me alone.

David Cassidy singing to me.

I think about it for three seconds.

Me – No thanks.

I can't disappoint that optimistic, frothy fourteen-year-old Dawn. What if this older David turns out to be a raddled old grumpy lizard? It would break my raddled old grumpy heart. I can't risk it. So I politely decline.

Twat or not?

I still don't know.

———————— ✳ ————————

I sincerely wish I'd taken my own advice on another occasion more recently.

Here's the thing, OK?

I love Norah Jones.

I love her album *Come Away with Me.*

It's one of those albums that was seminal for me. We all have them, don't we? – an album that was perhaps the accompanying soundtrack to some important and, for me, difficult years. The music comes to signify the comfort it was, the album is almost your friend, who speaks your innermost feelings so accurately, and more eloquently than you ever can. You can develop a kind of ownership, due to the connection you feel with the music and the musician.

I certainly felt this link with Norah.

Not in a weird way.

But I certainly DID feel like we had a sort of sisterhood going on, an affinity of sorts.

So – it was in this spirit that I bought tickets to see her perform in concert at the Hammersmith Apollo about sixteen years ago. The concert was sublime. I was a bit miffed that I had to share her with 2,000 other people, but I was quickly over that irritation when I could've sworn that a couple of times in the evening, she seemed to be looking DIRECTLY at me, singing both about me and to me. Yep. Norah and me.

Somewhere in the second half of the concert, there was a sweet moment where Norah told us that her shoes were hurting her, that they were too tight. She asked us if we minded if she just kicked them off?

Of course not, darling girl, you do that.

Mi casa su casa.

I became one of those loud, boundary-less people I so detest, when I found myself shouting, 'You go, girl! Be comfortable! Yeah!'

– probably the most motherly of all heckles.

Anyhoo, she did indeed kick off her shoes and for the rest of the show she was delightfully barefoot.

Lovely.

I woke the next morning, thinking about MY NEW BEST FRIEND NORAH JONES. I was ruminating about what her life must be like when she's on tour. Is she homesick? Tired? What is her life like at home? Where is home, actually?

I have no idea where she lives or how she lives, but I drift off into a flight of fancy. I imagine she lives in a Boho-ish community. In somewhere called . . . what? Singertown maybe. It's probably nestled in amongst some big gentle hills in . . . where? Virginia or somewhere like that. She lives on a ranch, I decide, because I reckon she has tons of rescue animals she gives sanctuary to, because she's such a good soul. She's likely got chickens and donkeys, possibly some llamas and a big ol' blind hound lolloping about. We have to be careful about what we feed him because he gets a gippy tummy if he eats anything sweet, so I'm always careful not to give him a corner of my oatcake honey brownie that Norah bakes. I love those. I love being there on the ranch. Norah's always relaxed there. She wanders about with a sarong on, no shoes obvs. She cooks . . . oh, I dunno . . . halloumi pittas for us all. Delish.

I especially love the evenings there, because Noo (my nickname for her) invites all her muso mates over and we sit around the fire pit as the sun goes down, and they've got their guitars and harmonicas and . . . triangles out and we just make sweet music all together and I join in with the singing. I magically know the lyrics and I harmonize easily and Noo turns to me and says,

Norah – Hey Dawn (in an American accent), you can REALLY sing!

Me – Oh stop it, Noo, no really, stop it, YOU are the singer, not me. But . . . y'know . . . thanks.

It's GORGEOUS . . .

ANYWAY – back in reality. I'm remembering what happened with the shoes onstage the night before. I see that she has another concert that night at the Apollo. It's a two-night run. My fuddled thick brain started to fizz with ideas as to how I can genuinely make Norah Jones be my new best friend for real.

PING! Bright idea.

I know exactly what to do.

I'm going to buy her some wondrous new shoes and deliver them directly into her hands and then, surely, she will love me...?

Now, French, think – what is Norah's shoe-vibe? Would she like some moccasins maybe? Or some kitten-heels? I'm not sure, but I head out to Portobello and Notting Hill. There are loads of amazing shoe shops there and they're all alarmingly expensive. When she sees the box and realizes where they've come from, she'll know the commitment and investment I've made in both the shoes and our future friendship. Surely that will ignite the flame...? She might even have a little tear and a hug and probably she'll invite me to watch the show again, but this time from the side of the stage where she can have me in her eyeline at all times. She will definitely dedicate a song to me.

No doubt about that.

I have decided at this point that she's a size 5. Like me. Well, of course, that's going to come in handy when we want to share shoes on holiday and such.

So – I go into an intimidating shop in Notting Hill and I buy a beautiful pair of size 5 flats. Ouch. They are really expensive. I head towards the stage door of the Apollo. It's early evening. She will surely be in there by now. Sound-checking or something. I've worked at this theatre many times and I'm hoping beyond hope that the stage door man remembers me. I'm giving him my whole face of teeth smile in a desperate attempt to be recognized. It's genuinely disgusting.

Of course, he doesn't know me.

Predictable.

Man – What do you want?

Me – Hello. Yes. I have something for Norah.

Man – Wait here. I'll call for the manager.

Bugger. This is a hurdle.

An officious woman turns up. I've forgotten her name; I seem to have blocked her out of my memory quite effectively.

Officious Manager Woman – Yep? What is it?

Me – Hello. Yes. I have something for Norah?

Officious Manager Woman – Agh God. No! Tell me it's not shoes. Everyone's brought her shoes.

Me (blindsided) – No, it's NOT shoes ... it's ... it's ... well, yes, it's shoes ...

Officious Manager Woman – Oh God. Come with me.

She's rude, but at least I'm getting in the building and now I'm following her through corridors to Norah where the love story can finally begin.

I follow her.

We don't go to Norah.

We go to a room – she opens the door – it is stacked from floor to ceiling with unopened boxes of brand-new shoes presumably from Norah's adoring fans.

This is THE MOMENT.

I AM FORCED TO REALIZE that perhaps I'm not that precious and special to Norah Jones.

In fact . . .

If I'm honest (hard) . . .

She doesn't know me at all.

Right.

I get it.

I leave very quickly, mumbling repeatedly under my breath:

Twat. Twat. Twat. Twat. Twat.

You'd think I might learn something profound about myself and my pathetic needs.

You'd think I might stop crushing on certain individuals.

Yeah – think on.

KAE TEMPEST

This is possibly one of my saddest examples of such behaviour, and it happened very RECENTLY.

I take Kae Tempest personally.

I have read their words, listened to their performances and felt a thunderingly visceral connection. It's a mixture of admiration and devotion. I especially respect wordsmiths; I appreciate an adroit composition of words more than pretty much any other art form. If I hear or read poetry that wakes me up or resonates with me, it is honestly more of a thrill than anything else I know.

It's better than rollercoasters

It's better than wine

It's better than swimming

It's better than my best bra

It's as good as kissing

It's as good as dogs

It's as good as down there

It's just like love.

When a poet nails your feelings to a T, it somehow validates you in an extremely potent way.

I can't claim to understand everything Kae speaks and writes of, but I'm willing to swim in the slipstream of their words until I do. In the meantime, they make me feel some extraordinary, forgotten, instinctive stuff again, and I'm so grateful for that.

So I'm a fan.

A big fat fan.

Solidly.

Really, I should just leave it at that, but my patent need for too intimate a connection reared its ugly head again. I think it might be to do with greed. I want more of what I like. I think it also might have to do with approval. I want them to favour me. I think it also might have to do with discipleship. I want to be included in amongst an inner sanctum of devotees.

All of this is RIDICULOUS, and I know it, but my compulsion to step closer in to be under the warmth of Kae's potential aegis kicked in.

Kae had a gig in Bristol.

That was the closest show to me, in Cornwall, of the long list of their tour dates.

I'd never seen them live, save a bit of Glastonbury on the telly. That was good . . . but . . . I was longing to be in the same air as Kae and their words.

They had a new work, *The Line is a Curve*, and this is what would be performed at the Marble Factory with the phenomenal Hinako Omori on keyboards.

I bought two tickets.

Then I realized that I didn't want to go WITH anyone. I wanted to soak it up alone. I'd never ever done that before. Go to a gig alone? Not usual for me. I also realized that it was a standing gig. I have a crumbling left knee (more of that anon) and can't stand for long.

I made a decision to ask my PA Lovely Sue to contact Kae's folks to ask if I could sit somewhere. (I've been lucky enough to sit next to the sound desk at my darlin' Alison Moyet gigs before now and I wondered if they'd let me do that?) I was praying they didn't think I was being a presumptuous demanding diva. I was hoping it didn't ruin my chances of a possible face-to-face snatched moment with Kae . . . ?

I knew that was unlikely, but I couldn't staunch the hope.

The raw and needy hope.

I booked into a hotel in Bristol, alone.

Odd.

I organized a car to the gig.

I listened endlessly to the album.

I knew it.

It was under my skin . . .

'My skin's your skin . . .'

'. . . leaves, rain . . .'

'Sometimes it passes . . .'

'. . . keep breathing . . .'

'I'll fight you till I win . . .'

'More pressure, More release . . .'

It was mine.

Alone.

I arrived at the back door of the gig and was shown to a chair (phew!) at the side of the stage, a slightly elevated platform, a closed-off area all to myself.

I could see EVERYTHING.

A kind man brought me a drink.

I was in heaven. I was ready.

Heart. Beat. Fast.

Then it happened.

Kae came on stage.

The Line is a Curve happened in the same room as me.

OK, there were many hundreds of others, all swaying with the hypnotic rhythm and witnessing the phenomenon, but for me – it was revelatory, it was PERSONAL.

'Please use me,

Please move through me ...

Let me be love ...'

Yes, Kae. You are. And I felt it.

They were in their flow.

And I was alongside, swept up.

It was glorious.

I couldn't help how much I wanted to meet Kae, I longed to tell them about how they mattered to me so much. And why.

I wanted to tell them quietly. Privately.

I'd been told someone would come and collect me at the end to take me to them.

I was electric with excitement.

I waited after the audience left.

A lady (I think she was French) approached me . . .

Lady – Hello. You are Dawn, yes? I'm afraid that Kae cannot see you today. There are Covid restrictions, we are protecting the show, not even family can visit backstage, so sorry.

Me – Of course, no problem, thank you.

And that was it.

Kae and I were not to know each other.

I was inside out gutted.

I was so ready to love them with all my being.

I ordered my cab to come earlier.

I slipped away.

I went to my hotel room.

I wept like a baby.

I had nowhere to put my feelings.

I didn't like how much of a spoiled brat I was behaving.

It's not my inalienable right to wedge myself into the life of anyone. I don't own them, no one does. It's needy and entitled to think so.

I know that, thank you.

But the fact remains that I love them and to this day I still want to wallop a big dollop of it on them. Not in a violent way.

What the cocking hell is wrong with me?

I'VE GOT TO STOP BEING SUCH A MASSIVE FANATICAL GROUPIE TWAT!

Just watch the show, French, and let the artist be.

MADONNA

On the subject of idols, I just can NOT leave Madonna out.

Anyone who watched even one episode of *French and Saunders* back in the day will know that we had a simmering obsession. So did everyone else, I suppose.

She is the same age as us.

Her meteoric rise and her remarkable, versatile, multi-discipline stellar career happened alongside our considerably gentler and smaller journey, timewise. We longed to have her on our show, and we invited her repeatedly, to no avail. It's as if she was busy or something . . . ?

No matter. We still adored her.

It became a tradition to ask her, receive the customary rejection and then we could get on with making our show. She was our talisman in a way. Her refusal became our good luck. And of course, as so often happened with 'guests' on F&S, if you decided not to turn up, then you were fair game. We had a lot of harmless fun at her expense, even using the shouting of her name.

'MADONNA! MADONNA!' was the nearest thing to a catchphrase we ever managed.

We were cheeky but, I hope, never unkind.

Somewhere along the way, Jennifer actually met her. It must've been when she was working in the USA.

I didn't.

But I really wanted to.

So, I was in Melbourne on tour with my show *30 Million Minutes*, and Madonna happened to be touring at the same time. This was 2016.

We had the same promoter, who let me know that Madonna was doing a semi-secret small show one evening in between her big stadium gigs. The only problem was that the start time was 8.30 p.m. I would still be doing my own show across town. He assured me she was always late, especially with a little private show like this, so I raced over to their theatre as soon as I came off stage. I arrived about 10.30 p.m., sure that I would've missed a chunk of it, but no such thing.

We waited.

We waited.

At 1.30 a.m. the next morning, she finally graced the stage.

It was genuinely one of the most surreal moments of my life.

The crowd were quite drunk. I was not, I wanted to be sharp to see this. I'd been told this was Madonna in her 'comedian' mode . . .

THIS. I. HAVE. TO. SEE.

She came onstage dressed as a sexy clown, in full white face.

She was on a tiny trike, which squeaked as she pedalled it to the front of the stage. Curious.

The next hour left me with my jaw agape.

She told bad jokes. On purpose. That was her schtick. She called us all 'motherfuckers' for not laughing. She sang a few songs with a pared-down tiny group of musos and backing singers, all also in full clown garb. Designer clown garb.

It was mighty odd.

Nothing quite landed, but I massively admired her gusto and her chutzpah to give it a go.

When the strange show was over, bearing in mind it was by now about 3 a.m. or later, the promoter invited us to come and meet Madonna.

I was with my tour manager Adam.

Although it was late, and bearing in mind that I'm a cuppa tea and tucked up by 11 p.m.-type o' gal, especially if I'm on tour, I couldn't turn down the chance to meet the goddess, however strange the night had been. This chance would probably never come again.

We followed a stage manager to a space below and backstage where he sat us on a sofa in amongst the melee of Madonna's crew and band, and he told us she'd be out to see us shortly. It was a circus of odd bods buzzing about, madly.

We waited.

We waited over an hour.

It was now something like 4.30 a.m.

I had a show that same night.

I whispered to Adam that perhaps we should simply slip away . . . ?

At which point Madonna was suddenly there, right in front of me.

I jumped up.

We were face to face.

Up close, she looked pretty alarming because she still had all the cakey white make-up on.

I was meeting a feisty ghost-clown.

Madonna — Hi. We've met before.

(We hadn't. I would've remembered that.)

Me — I don't think so.

Madonna — Yes. We have.

Me — OK.

I was pathetically acquiescent. If she said so, then it must be so.

Madonna — What did you think?

Christ! My inner world ground to a halt. I had SO MUCH to say about how I might think this show could be so much better – but who the cock am I to tell her anything? Even about comedy? It's at moments like this that you should really step into your power, your truth and your position as an equal human being, both together on the same planet in the same moment. But we don't.

We cave.

It's polite.

And it's 4.30 a.m.

Me – It was . . . lovely . . . in many interesting and challenging ways . . .

We meet again, my twatness.

Madonna gave me a withering look. The type that says, 'No, thanks, not my kinda person.'

She said a civil goodbye.

She walked on.

I retreated ASAP back to a world I understand.

A world of mates and biscuits and teasing

and normal and twat.

And ... breathe.

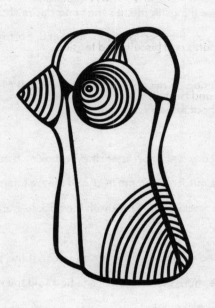

MAMMA MIA!

No one has ever asked me to be in a musical. It's almost as if they think I can't sing, or something. I just can't fathom it?

Like so many things in life, it's that one desire that's just out of reach, denied you, that occupies your hanker department entirely.

Try then to imagine my delirium when my agent Maureen called me one day about fifteen years ago.

Maureen – Love, hello, now listen: they're making a new film version of the hit stage musical *Mamma Mia!* and they're interested in you to play the funny, wacky one, y'know, with the back-to-front hat . . .

(I had no idea who she was referring to as, at this point, I hadn't seen the stage show, but no matter, she had said the word 'musical' – that's all the bait I needed.)

Maureen – Love, Meryl Streep's on board. They're filming it in Greece this summer . . .

Right. I've died of joy. This is the job of dreams. Plus, Meryl Streep is about to become my new best friend . . .

AMAAAZING!

This is the music of Abba.

This is me in a musical.

At last. At very long last.

So, I'm invited to meet the producers the very next day and we have a lovely, happy meeting over a posh cream tea (#jamfirstnoexceptions). We talk about the story, the character, the whole exuberance of it. It's a female-fronted story with lots of wonderful parts for women of various ages.

They are offering me the part.

I'm giddy with delight.

It's all perfect.

But I want to be as honest as possible:

Me – Look, this is fantastic, but I just want to put it out there – I'm not a trained singer or anything. Least, not professionally trained, but I can hold a note and I would love to do this.

Them – Honestly, it doesn't matter, really. Most of the actors aren't singers, so we are prepared for that. The two men from Abba . . .

(I'm trying to remember their names – I should know this . . . is it Bejink and Bejonk?)

. . . they've got a couple of knobs . . .
    (I think we knew that.)

. . . and however bad the singing is, they can magically re-tune it. So, seriously, don't worry about that, it's gonna be fine. We got you covered.

Me – Right, well, that's a relief to know. But . . . I'm not sure you'll need that because I CAN keep in tune and of course, I know and LOVE, excuse me, this music. So. Yes. I'd love to be a part of it.

I leave the meeting full of happiness and sandwiches and scones and cream. Rarely have I been so sated.

Maureen called me pretty quickly by way of a follow-up.

Maureen – Love, sounds like that went well. They're on board. One tiny thing – it's just a formality, nothing to worry about, but they'd love you to meet the musical director. Y'know, simply to trot you through some of the songs you'll be singing in the film, just to familiarize yourself. Tomorrow morning, Palace Theatre.

No problem. Looking forward to it.

I tip up at the Palace Theatre in Cambridge Circus at the appointed time, and the offices where the meeting is due to take place are right at the top of the building, four flights up. I'm feeling sprightly so:

I race up the first flight of stairs.

Tippety, Toppity, up we go, light as a feather.

I dash up the second flight.

Tippety, Toppity, Tippety, Toppity, up we go, but heavier now.

I walk up the third flight.

Tippety, Toppity, Clumpety, Cloppity, up we go, quite hard now.

I crawl up the fourth flight.

Clumpety, Cloppity, Puffety, Panty, up we go, nearly dead.

Come on, French! Keep breathing. You need to be alive to get this job, no one wants an old, conked-out mare in their jolly film. Stand up, get your breath back. It was way too ambitious, that optimistic approach to those stairs. Calm down now. You're too stoked. It's not a good look. Get it together. Gather yourself. Breathe, two, three, four . . . steady, steady.

You want this job.

A lot.

I eventually regulate my breathing. I'm ready. I knock on the door and enter a large room and I'm suddenly in my favourite kind of atmosphere, because this is a sea of gay men. They are all tapping away at their computers until they see me, when, as one, they screech at me. It's a huge, warm, wonderful, camp welcome.

Me – Thank you, guys! Thanks for all the encouragement. It's so good, thank you, thank you.

Greek chorus of marvellous gay men – It's gonna be fine! You'll knock it out of the park!

Fingers crossed! Go girl! Go for it, Dawneeeee!

Along comes the musical director, a jaunty chap with a huge smile. He hives me off into a little side room where the piano is and he invites me to 'squish in' next to him on the piano stool and, after a bit of frothy banter to relax us, he says,

MD – Don't worry, everything will be fine. I'm going to start and you just jump in whenever you like, OK?

Me – Perfect. Lovely. Here we go, off to Abbatown. Ding! Ding!

He starts to plonk away enthusiastically, and it reminds me of Bobby Crush. The song is 'Money, Money, Money'. I know it. As I'm drawing breath, I realize I've missed the first musical cue. No matter, I'll catch the next one, when it comes round . . .

MD – In your own time.

Me – Yep, yep, here we go . . .

Still I don't start. He plays the same refrain again . . .

He resorts to counting me in . . . I'm back in kindergarten.

MD – And . . . ? Two, three, four . . . ?

I do it. I start singing.

What comes out of my mouth is nothing earthly. It's not recognizable as singing at all. It's definitely a noise, but it's a visceral sound of pain and despair and has very little, if nothing whatsoever, to do with the actual tune. It's a long, long way away from it. It's on a different planet to the song. I also can't seem to settle on any key that's familiar in music on earth. It might, at a push, resonate with the throat singers of remote Mongolia, but it's not a technique I know well enough to debut here, at my important audition. I'm making guttural squawking sounds that are awakening krakens. The MD stops me, mercifully.

MD – Don't worry, lots of people get a bit nervous if they're not used to singing.

Me – Yes, right. Sorry. I'm not sure what happened there. I just stayed on one note, didn't I? More like an offensive din. Sorry!

MD – No prob. Let's have another go . . . you'll know this one . . .

I knew the last one. It doesn't bode well. He starts the next song. It's 'Take a Chance on Me'.

COME ON, FRENCH!

I gulp.

I start.

It's worse.

Not only have I forgotten what singing is, I don't even comprehend what WORDS are any more.

At best, I sound like a dying cow, a beast of burden yowling at the moon in the final throes of life.

At worst, it's genuinely sinister. The noise is coming from deep down inside me, a place I hitherto didn't know existed. A cavern in my lungs where Beelzebub keeps his shrieking demons wet and furious, and now they're escaping through all of my front face holes. Including my nostrils.

It is properly awful.

I'm out of control.

It sounds like I'm possessed.

I am.

I'm possessed.

The Gods of flounder are inhabiting me.

Me (shouting over the piano) – Sorry! Ha ha ha! Sorry. I can sing much better than this – this just isn't me at all.

MD (shouting back) – Don't give up. Try this one. We'll get there!

He launches into 'Mamma Mia'. Everyone in the known universe knows this song. It's the title of the cockin' film, for heaven's sake . . .

I ramp it up. It's my only choice at this moment.

There has been a mutiny on my body ship. I'm no longer the captain. I'm not even in the galley cutting up limes to avoid scurvy.

I'm not in the engine room, helping to keep the motors running.

I'm certainly not at the helm, steering.

I am a bilge pump, desperately trying, and failing, to fire up to avert the steady sinking.

The sound emanating from me is genuinely the worst thing I've ever heard.

It's hurting both sets of ears in the room.

It's a living torment.

Of behemoth proportions.

Fortunately, he surrenders at this point and stops playing. With a sympathetic smile and an understanding tilt of the head, he delivers this devastating invitation to leave:

MD – Well, it's been lovely to meet you.

To which I reply feebly:

Me – You're welcome.

I exit the torture chamber swiftly, all the while grinning gormlessly. It isn't my intent to gurn like this, but my lips are stuck to my teeth in an unfortunate and ugly rictus grimace of nervous horror.

I re-enter the lovely, welcoming room again, only to find every single person with their heads down in their work. Nobody, but NOBODY, will look me in the eye. They are paralysed with vicarious shame.

They heard it all, didn't they?

I have no ally. Not one. I don't deserve one. I've just murdered their favourite music babies one by one in the cruellest way.

I'm shunned.

I attempt a pathetic:

Me – Bye then. Seeya.

Nothing.

Me – No? Right. It's a firm no.

I fling open the door and race down the stairs, out into the lovely fresh air. The street is thronging with people who've never heard me sing. These are my type of people. Ear virgins. A fresh start with humans who know no better. Or rather, worse.

I'm dripping with embarrassment, but I'm busy reassuring myself that it won't matter because they can fix it all. It'll be all right.

My phone rings. It's Maureen. It's barely been a minute.

Maureen – Love, it's not going to work out, I'm afraid. Just not the right fit . . .

Me – And my singing was appalling.

Maureen – And your singing was appalling, yes.

Me – But what about Bejink and Bejonk? They told me they can sort it out. With knobs . . . ? However awful . . . ?

There follows a silence as long as the longest last gasp at life. Has Maureen died of shame?

Eventually . . . after a century of wait . . .

Me – Maureen? You still there?

Maureen – Can I just reiterate, love. Your singing was appalling . . .

So.

Enter the sublime Julie Walters.

Poised. Talented. Confident. Funny.

IN TUNE.

Not a twat.

Gotta hand it to her.

Albeit with a clenched fist.

Still, as with so many moments in my life, if you reject me, however justified, from something I really want to do:

I do my own twatty version.

Cut to: Comic Relief 2009

Fatty as Meryl Streep

Lumley as the tall one

Me as Julie Walters

Sienna Miller as Sophie

Alan Carr as Colin Firth

Philip Glenister as Pierce Brosnan

A Swede as The Swede

Miranda Hart as The Director

Matt Lucas as The Choreographer

Mel and Sue as The Producers

RESULT!

MORE TWATLETS

MUSICAL INSTRUMENTS

OK, everyone in the UK who went to school in the sixties/seventies learnt to play the recorder. It was pretty much mandatory, and it was an aural abuse for both the player and the listener. If ever there was an effective deterrent to keep children well away from learning an instrument, this was it. I think I mastered 'Three Blind Mice' and 'Twinkle Twinkle Little Star' along with everyone else, but I couldn't wait to stop playing it.

A similar experience happened with the piano. I was at boarding school, so there was a piano in the hall that we had access to in the evenings. One of my chums showed me how to play the basics of 'Für Elise' (which I always thought was called 'Fleur a Lees' – 'less flowers'(?!)).

Again, everyone learnt this.

Or at least the first few bars, which are the simplest.

The story of the tune is that Beethoven wrote this piece for a student he fell in love with. She wasn't the best piano student, so he made the beginning really easy for her. After he discovered she was engaged, he was miffed and made sure the ending was so tricky that she'd never be able to play it. Hmm. Vindictive much, Beethoven?

So, I played two bars of 'Für Elise' and 'Chopsticks' over and over again, ad nauseam, hoping that my fingers would magically understand how to work a piano. I hoped I might be a sudden savant and be instantly accomplished.

Shockingly, that didn't happen.

Unbelievably, I didn't progress AT ALL.

I know.

In my teens, I decided it would be cool to learn to play the bass guitar. I was obsessed with an all-female US rock band called Fanny (I know) at the time and I knew it would be major boy bait if I could play. I saved up all my odd-jobs money (I tried to convince my mother that 'cleaning out the guinea-pig hutch' was a pay-worthy job. She reminded me that they were MY guinea pigs, that I'd begged to have. Good point, well made) and found an unloved Framus Bass guitar and amp in a second-hand shop. The fretboard was narrow and therefore good for smaller hands. I believe Bill Wyman used to play such a guitar?

I brought it home.

I plugged it in.

I couldn't read music.

I had no idea how to play it.

It sounded AWFUL.

Yet again, I was shocked that I wasn't instantly miraculously marvellous at it.

But . . .

I was extremely good at posing with it. I knew how to LOOK like I was playing it. Sometimes I would put on loud records and 'play' along. Status Quo was best for this. There are only ever three chords in any of their songs and so they're easier to fake it to. I have photos, which I think I persuaded my poor mum to take, where I am furiously posing, and firmly believing that I look uncannily like a member of Fanny on an album cover.

Anyone who saw these photos might well have believed I could play and, apparently, that's what mattered most.

Twat.

Something similar happened with the saxophone, except I was in my twenties and should, by rights, have grown out of the silly posing by then, surely. I mentioned to a then-boyfriend that I wanted to learn a) how to read music and b) how to play the saxophone. I didn't mean it. I was showing off. I was a bit shocked when he bought me a brand-new, and very expensive, saxophone for my birthday. I'd never seen anything quite so beautiful when I opened the case. I resolved to finally do it. Stop posing and actually learn.

Did I?

Did I hell.

I regularly took it out of the case and put it together the best way I could. Was the mouthpiece facing the wrong way? No idea.

Then – I would hold it and look at myself holding it in the mirror, trying to recreate UB40 and Madness poses. I even tried to imitate the uber-cool Stan Getz.

I was quite good at it.

The *looking* like I was playing.

I didn't raise a single note on that instrument.

Several years later, I donated it to a young chum who expressed an interest in actually playing it. I felt sorry for the instrument. It deserved a home with a real person, rather than a twat.

RED LIPSTICK

The twattery in this story is shared between myself and a lovely make-up artist friend I have called Gill.

I had to do a photo shoot for the poster of a panto I was going to be in at the Palladium. I was rehearsing something else at the University in Falmouth, so they sent the costume and the photographer down to me there. My character was Dame Trot, Jack's mother in *Jack and the Beanstalk*, and the outfit was full-on aged milkmaid with a mob cap. I'd asked for a purple wig, which duly arrived along with the whole ensemble, but I needed help to get it on and get made up.

Enter Gill. An old chum who lived nearby and is very experienced.

We decided together to go for a fairly glam make-up look with big false eyelashes, etc. to achieve a vaguely MILF look (milkmaid I'd like to... be friends with). This meant rosy cheeks and strong fuchsia-pink lips.

Gill had acquired some new make-up from a company she works with, and was keen to use their products, which were all in a fancy-pants bag with the company logo on the side.

She fished out the foundation and the eyeshadows, etc., and we cracked on with it. Of course, we were mainly malicious gossiping, so we were a bit behind when the photographer came to get a rough ETA (which is photographer-speak for 'Get a move on!').

I asked Gill where the lip liner was, and she told me it was in the bottom of said bag. I fished about and found it, a strong pink as requested, in an interesting pen-like tube. Effective packaging, I thought. We were rushing, so I applied the line as she looked on. A good bold colour and a distinct outline. We liked it so much we filled the whole lip area in with it and it looked perfect.

We ran to the set and did the photos, spit-spot, in no time at all.

Everyone was happy. This photo would be slotted into the group cast on the poster when everyone had done their individual photos.

The photographer packed up and left, as did the costume makers with the costume, which left Gill and me getting the wig and make-up off.

I used cotton pads and make-up remover as per usual . . . but the lip colour was refusing to budge, which was odd.

I scrubbed and scrubbed, but it remained.

I picked up the lip-liner container and took a closer look at it.

The label said: 'Sign Pen – pure liquid ink – permanent marker'.

Oh. My. Chuffing. God. We'd just used an actual PEN on my lips. The company must've left it in the bottom of the bag whilst fulfilling the order . . .

It remained that bright pink, for two whole weeks.

I had the mouth of a baboon's arse, and I deserved it, frankly.

DANNY DYER

In March 2023, Fatty and I did a parody of *The Traitors* TV show for Comic Relief. Claudia Winkleman joined in and the whole thing was a blast. Lots of different 'celebs' came out to play and sat around the famous big table.

Danny Dyer was there. I'd not met him before, but I'm a fan.

I weighed in with:

Me – Hi Danny. Thanks for doing this.

Danny – No prob.

Me – Hey, something I wanted to say to you, actually (ingratiating). I have a niece who's working in the art depart on 'Enders (too familiar), so maybe you can keep an eye out for her? She's so lovely . . . (I'm floundering) and we've got to encourage young people to come into the industry, haven't we? (Literally don't know what I'm talking about now, I'm just blethering.) So, praps, if you see her, you can just say hello. I'm not suggesting you go looking for her or anything, just if you bump into each other . . . (shut up, French, stop using words) but then, you don't know what she looks like, do you? Well, she looks like a younger, better me. Ha ha. Look out for that!

I run out of blether and eventually, mercifully, grind to a halt. There's an uneasy pause. Everyone is looking at me. Why?

Danny – You do realize I left *EastEnders* at Christmas?

Me – Ummmmmm . . . did you?

Danny – Yeah. Quite a big exit. Main story . . .

Me – Right. Ummm . . .

Danny laughs, he's a total gent, and I die a thousand deaths. There is no way back. Everyone there has witnessed my sycophantic idiocy, cast and crew alike.

So, as is the case in arse-wrenching moments like this, we all just pretend it hasn't happened. La la la.

Sorry, Danny. I'm just a twat.

A COAT AND A KIMONO

I went to Venice for a wedding anniversary with the first Mr French. It was about 1988, I think. There were many, many beautiful shops. Clothes shops. Designer clothes shops. I've never really spent time or money in these kinds of shops because there is nothing in there that fits me.

Well, possibly a bag. At a stretch. A stretchy bag. Nothing else.

So, these kinds of shops are alienating and intimidating for me.

I avoid them.

But I was in Venice, full of romance and optimism, and in a moment of spontaneous madness, I made the giant mistake of casually crossing the threshold into one of these exclusive boutiques.

I immediately knew it was a fatal misjudgement. A lanky string bean of a person dressed in minimal black started to follow me around the shop. I knew she thought I might be about to steal something, I just knew it.

I felt criminal.

I felt guilty.

Then I felt angry.

Then I felt murderous.

All the while, I was determinedly flicking through endless clothes that would truthfully only fit a child. I glanced at her. She glowered at me. I pointedly continued with the defiant flicking through the rails. In fact, I slowed down. On purpose. I looked at EVERY SINGLE ITEM in that awful shop.

I could feel her judgey eyes boring into my back. She hated me, and my type. Unsightly tubbies, ruining the sleek aesthetic of her shop.

Although I was mainly furious, I also felt humiliated. I knew I wasn't the correct 'type' to be in this place.

It was an audacity that I was in here in my scruffy bad clothes, carrying my déclassé pleather bag.

My mindset shifted.

Fuck her.

I'm going to buy something, and I'm going to do it with aplomb.

What could I buy?

My eyes desperately darted about and finally settled on the prize.

The only solitary item of clothing in that store that would fit me – a huge, wrap-around cashmere coat in a very sophisticated gun-metal grey.

I took it from the rack.

I didn't look at the tag.

I didn't try it on.

I looked the string bean right in the eye and flumped it down in front of her, by the till.

I didn't ask '*Quanto costa?*'

A confident rich bitch doesn't do that.

I flicked my credit card down.

I didn't lose eye contact for a second.

She needed to understand that I was Queen of all I surveyed in her shitty shop.

She didn't scare me.

Hell no.

Take my money.

I briefly saw the price as I signed the receipt (it was the old days, folks), but it was in lire (it was the old days, folks), so the dizzying number of noughts was impossible to compute or convert quickly.

It didn't matter.

I was standing firmly in my defiance, I wasn't going to budge.

She wrapped it and put it into a big posh bag with long rope handles.

I swept out of that shop, victorious. That'll teach her for being snobby.

I raced back to the hotel.

I speedily did the sums, as my heart threatened to pump me to a quick death . . .

I'd paid more for this coat than I earned as a teacher for an entire year only seven years before.

I didn't have this kind of money to spare.

I paid it off for three years, gradually, on my maxed-out credit card.

I LOVED the coat, and I wore it a lot . . . but . . . there's bravado . . . and there's being a twat.

A similar lunacy occurred when I was wandering around Bath about ten years ago.

There seriously ought to be a sort of Samaritans' helpline for gullible eejits like me. Maybe there could be a tracker on my phone that alerts a central control station anytime I'm entering a posh frock shop . . . or, as in this case, a vintage clothes emporium. Oh. No. The worst kind of temptation because, again, nothing vintage fits me, but I want it all so much that I lose all sense. Am I the only person who forgets my real life (which contains Wotsits and M&S knickers and bad leggings and tons of messy, unfinished crap) when I'm in a vintage shop, and decides I want to live a solidly fifties/sixties existence, head to toe, inside and out? I insert myself into an imaginary home, the like of which I don't own, which is decorated entirely by Twiggy or Audrey Hepburn. I resolve to start this new fantasy life immediately when I enter those dangerous shops, and I convince myself that whatever takes my fancy is my FIRST PURCHASE of a whole lifestyle change starting RIGHT THEN. It isn't. It never is.

Yet, I repeat this idiocy over and over and over again.

Anyhoo, on this particular occasion, a lovely helpful lady was showing me lots of gorgeous clothes, none of which were even close to my size.

Yet again, I ended up narrowing my search down to not what I loved, but what would fit. Or even go over my head.

She had a lightbulb moment and steered me to the rear of the shop, where very precious items were kept.

There, in amongst many treasures, in a special box, wrapped in tissue, she showed me a kimono-style dressing gown in a beautiful silk William Morris design. This kimono had a Liberty label in it.

Vintage Liberty.

William Morris patterning.

This time, I *did* look at the tag. It was an eye-watering figure. Over a thousand pounds. Utterly ridiculous for me to even consider.

Would I even wear it? Probably not, it was so delicate and special.

Why pay such a huge amount to hang something in a wardrobe?

I had the strength to say:

Me – Hmm, yes, it's really lovely, but I'm going to have to think about it . . .

Nice Lady – Of course. Remember, it's very rare, and I'm afraid I can't guarantee to keep it back for you. If someone else was interested, I'd have to . . . y'know.

Me – Of course, of course, I totally understand.

I left the shop thinking she was a bit cheeky to say that, but it was probably at least the truth, and she was a nice, helpful, friendly lady, unlike the Venetian Lilith.

I went back to my hotel, hoping to forget the whole incident.

But no . . .

I left Bath to drive home, hoping that would perish all thoughts.

But no . . .

This ruddy kimono occupied every inch of my waking life. I tried to eject it, but it returned, begging me to rescue it from its box in the back of that shop, insisting that I imagine myself floating about in it in my home, like Norma Desmond.

Ludicrous money.

I can't possibly.

Obscene.

Wrong.

But . . . oh, so beautiful.

Plus . . . it's my first purchase of my brand-new, retro-style life, where EVERYTHING is going to be beautiful and different, isn't it, so I might as well push the boat out in style. I'm going to be an Art Deco/Nouveau (Which? Dunno) kind of floaty, arty goddess-sort of person from now on, so this KIMONO is vital.

Necessary.

Unmissable.

What if someone else is in there right now purchasing it?

No. That mustn't happen.

I need it.

I can't live without it.

My life will be worthless if I don't get it.

At this point, a primitive, ugly, wanton greed possessed me and I called the shop.

Me – Hi, is the kimono safe?

Nice Lady – Yes. You only left an hour ago.

Me – I know . . . but . . . I needed to know.

Nice Lady – Would it help if we could manage a discount?

Me (shouting, gasping, desperate) – Yes. Yes, please.

Nice Lady – How about five per cent off . . . ?

Me (without thinking) – YES! YES! Deal. I'll send a cheque now. Please don't sell it to anyone else. Please wrap it in children's hair and send it to me by way of Cottonwool Delivery Services immediately.

I worked out that the discount was minimal.

No matter. I was a certifiably crazed fool by then.

It arrived a few days later.

As I opened up the tissue to reveal it, the pangs of guilt and shame overwhelmed me.

However beautiful it was, and it is, I couldn't possibly face it every day.

I have a much-loved costume designer friend.

I knew she would love it.

She was turning sixty.

It was the perfect opportunity to turn my twatty greed into a joy.

LARK RISE

It's 2008, and I am offered the role of Caroline Arless in the TV drama series *Lark Rise to Candleford*, based on the ruddy gorgeous, semi-autobiographical novels by Flora Thompson, depicting country life where she grew up in Oxfordshire.

Caroline Arless is a 'free spirit', which is basically tellyspeak for 'drunk'. She was fun to play – reckless and mischievous. In our story, her husband was away at sea and she was struggling to raise their many kids.

I was well into my fifties when we made this show and was a bit alarmed when the producers suggested I'd have six or so kids, ranging from a twenty-year-old down to two babies on my hip. Really? In the olden days, I'd've probably been dead 'n' gone, never mind had tiny babies well past menopause. But, hey ho, they were writing the cheques, so who was I to argue the basic biological and historical logic?

The director very much wanted us to be relaxed as a family, so I was encouraged to have an open-door policy with my little caravan where we hung out waiting to do our scenes. I became friends with the kids, their parents and chaperones, and even with kids that weren't in our telly family. We ate together and played games and generally mucked about, so that we'd be natural together when the cameras were running. This was especially important for the babies, who can notoriously be difficult to manage on a set if they don't know you.

Amongst my kid-family were a brother and sister, Harry and Sophie Myles. I grew massively fond of them. Harry, in particular, became quite attached to me and was very physically close, always hugging me and holding my hand, bless him. It gradually became standard practice for him to be wrapped around me, one way or another, so much so that he was almost glued to me throughout the shooting day.

On one occasion, I walked across the set with Harry attached to me to talk to one of the other actors, and while we were yapping, she started to indicate to me, with wide-eyed alarm, to notice what Harry was up to . . .

I looked down at him. Harry was about nine or ten at this point and he was eye-level height with my giant bosoms, which were spilling out over the top of my far-too-tight corset. The producers had decided to dress me like some kind of ageing milkmaid for this part and the bosom-age was really bold. Very in your face.

Well, very in Harry's face!

As I glanced at him, he was mesmerized, staring at them, virtually with his tongue out. I basically had three bosoms: left one, right one and Harry.

I looked at his little face and it occurred to me that Harry was having some sort of preliminary awakening.

On me. Oh dear.

Harry was in his happy place, face to face with wibbly wobbly jubbly jibbly joy.

He was transfixed by the enormity and, let's face it, animated buoyant charms of the Frenchie norks.

Or maybe not.

Maybe . . . he was trapped in a nightmare of epic, bosomy proportions with my mammaries as the central horror.

Either way, I need to apologize, Harry, for failing to notice what was going on.

Luckily, I met up with Harry and his lovely sis Sophie recently. He seems relatively unscathed by it all. He has gone on to have a fruitful life and assures me he has developed a healthy respect for norks of all varieties.

WEE

Yes, sorry.

Feel free to skip these pages if tales of urinary misdemeanours aren't your bag. Personally, I think wetting your pants is usually a sign of having THE BEST TIME.

My pee pants moments have often been key times and therefore memorable.

I'm proud to say there are also many utterly forgettable pee pants moments that I won't be recounting here because I've forgotten them. More's the shame.

Anyhoo, off we go into the sodden world of piddle fun:

DIBLEY

I'm sure that on the day I die, the clip that will recur will be the puddle jump as Geraldine. We did it twice, actually. Richard wanted to reprise it since the response to the first one was so positive.

I remember when the art department, headed up by the fabulous Andrew Howe-Davies, built the hole in a back lane on a farm in Oxfordshire. They lowered a tank into the ground and put foam in the bottom of it for me to land on. The biggest problem was the temperature of the water. It was November, and so I would freeze if the water was cold, but if it was too warm, it would steam and that would be a giant giveaway. It had to be just right – which was a little bit warm.

Unfortunately, that was also the exact temperature at which a cold body relaxes – to the point of bladder slackening with no return.

As I entered the giant puddle, I also released my own secret warm contribution.

Not so secret now. Spoilt it for you.

Sorry.

TITANIC

Fatty Saunders and I didn't stint on the film parodies we did for *French and Saunders*. 'Titanic' was a case in point. Edgar Wright directed that sketch, Ade Edmondson played the tyrant director James Cameron, Jo Lumley narrated it and we played pretty much everyone else: the props masters, the extras and, of course, Leonardo DiCaprio and Kate Winslet. This sketch involved a LOT of water. It was always just behind or just in front, or around a corner.

The final scene involves Kate (Jen) lying on the wreckage of a door whilst Leo (me) clings on for dear life until he can hold on no longer and disappears backwards into the dark, salty depths of the ocean, gone forever.

In order to pull this off, we had to get into a proper huge water tank built especially for filming. I think it was at Shepperton film studios . . . ? I was in the water for most of the day. Up 'til lunchtime was no problem. AFTER lunch . . . mid-afternoon . . . AFTER a bottle of water . . . not so good.

Look, it was a long day and a huge tank of water and, as they say, always leave them something to remember you by.

Sorry.

THE PIANO

We had such a hoot doing this parody of the film starring Holly Hunter and Anna Paquin. We shot it in Littlehampton, if I remember rightly, and spent a lot of time on roller skates on the seafront.

The piddling moment happened when, in order to look like a child and half the height of Jennifer, the crew dug a hole in the sand for me to stand in. The second I stepped into it, I had a fit of the giggles because it was just so fantastically silly. I knew I ought to find a loo, but there was no public convenience nearby and I was wearing several layers of clothes, including thermal long johns to keep warm, with lacy bloomers over those, just like the little girl in the film. So – it would've been a total faff to find a toilet and I would hold up the filming for too long. I chose to stick it out and hope for herculean bladder control 'til the end of the day. Fatty knew I was in trouble with this dilemma, which of course prompted her to tease me with all kinds of stupid stuff. I couldn't move because I was buried up to my thighs. She did little dances, pulled faces, did impressions of all our regular favourites, including Madonna. I was laughing A LOT . . . but all pee remained safely in its rightful interior vessel.

Phew.

Until . . . the moment Russ Conway walked across the vast beach and sat down at the large crate containing said piano and started to cheerfully play one of his big hits, 'Side Saddle'.

He was looking right at us and grinning from ear to ear.

That was it.

I was helpless.

We'd written it, for dogs' sake. I knew what the gag was, but somehow in that very moment, I was seeing it for the first time and I was powerless to resist. It was hilarious and so I COULD NOT STOP LAUGHING.

The flood flaps opened, and I irrigated that beach. Liberally. With gusto.

And zero regret.

My only apologies were to the wardrobe department, who I think forgave me . . . ?

I will never ever forget the sopping joy of it all.

The delight.

And the drench.

And the drippy, cold, wet walk back up the beach at the end of the day, exhausted from howling so long and hard.

Happy incontinent days.

CONKING OUT

I clambered into the back of a black cab in London a couple of years ago.

Cabbie – Hi. Just to let you know, you're going to want to kiss me when you get out of this cab.

Me – Ummm, I don't think so, mate.

Cabbie – Yes. You are.

Me – Like your confidence, but . . . nah, thanks.

He then proceeded to tell me that he was the person who had, a few years prior, brought me round from a solidly thudding faint I'd experienced in a café when I was having a breakfast meeting with Richard Curtis about Comic Relief. I was mid-tour and fairly tired, but other than that, I have no answers for why I suddenly conked.

Poor Richard. He told me afterwards that he thought for a horrid brief moment I'd died.

I woke up on the floor, to a man pinching my ear and asking me if I knew where I was?

'How rude,' I thought.

For me, it felt for a few confusing moments that I was waking up from a lovely, long, deep sleep and this twat was in my bedroom disturbing it, so I was a bit (lot) grumpy.

Me – What are you doing? Get off me, you blaggard.

He kept asking questions until I realized what must've happened, and I was recovered enough to sit up.

An ambulance was called, and the two fab female medics inside checked all my 'vitals' and confirmed that I was indeed alive. I went on my merry way once I felt better.

I thanked the cabbie for his help back then, and he told me that he'd been a fireman in his past and was trained to bring people round with the ol' ear-pinching technique.

When I arrived at my destination, I did indeed, kiss him.

I've only ever fainted three times in my life. It's such a shocking experience that I remember all three.

The first-ever time was when my friend John came off his motorbike in Plymouth when we were teenagers. He wrapped himself around a lamppost and ruptured his spleen badly, so I went to visit him in hospital. I'm not great in hospitals. I temporarily turn into an extreme empath and start imagining what it would be like to be any single person I see. It's honestly ridiculous. I don't know why it happens, but I do know that it's exhausting, and I can't seem to stop myself.

So . . . I walked through the ward where he was to find him in the furthest bed, which of course meant that I'd already envisaged myself in about ten separate stages of horrific and catastrophic illness. I was quite wobbly by the time I reached his bed.

He looked so bad. Jaundiced and shocked. He was propped up in his bed with various tubes and cables disappearing into unimaginably awful places between the buttons of his pyjama top.

That was it.

I didn't even manage to say hello properly before I keeled over.

The next thing I knew, I was looking UP at the springs under his bed, with a kindly nurse trying to coax me back to consciousness. As I tried to get up, I realized, to my horror, that I was watering the floor, spending much more than a penny, spending a shilling, and not stopping. The nurse was benevolent:

Nurse – Don't worry about that, love, EVERYTHING relaxes when you faint, it's natural. We've got a mop, it's no problem.

I was mortified. I stood up and explained to poor John that I had to go. He hadn't said a single word. This was, frankly, a pretty shoddy visit from me. What a twat. No help to him at all.

As I walked back up the ward to the exit in my saturated trousers, leaving a snail trail of thin yellow wake behind me, the nurse offered me a plastic sheet to sit on on the bus.

Which was thoughtful.

If humiliating.

The final (mercifully) pee/faint story happened not long ago, when I finished a long and gruelling run of a pantomime at London's glittery Palladium. I honestly have LOVED being in both the pantos I've done there, but blimey, they are knackering because you are usually doing two shows a day. Sometimes seven days a week! I can't believe it's not illegal. Even if it is, it's lucrative and good fun, so who's complaining?

I am.

But only a bit.

I know.

Poor me.

Having a blast and getting paid well.

Who the cock do I think I am?

Anyhoo . . . I finished the run on a Sunday in mid-January and my husband bloke came up to London from Cornwall to help me load all my silly crap out of the dressing room ready to drive home for the first time in three months the next day.

We did two shows on that last day, so by the time we arrived back at the London flat, I was proper pooped.

And hungry.

So, we decided to nip round the corner to our local Thai restaurant for some quick noodles. As I sat down, my back started to ache, which was odd.

Even stranger was the fact that when the delicious food arrived, I took one look at it and knew I couldn't stomach it, for some reason. This is a giant red flag. I love food. I don't miss a meal, believe me.

Just as I tried to explain to my husband that I wasn't feeling so tickety-boo, I felt all the blood rush away from my head and that's the last I knew . . .

I conked.

I woke up with my head on his shoulder.

He informed me that I went spark out and collapsed like a sack of potatoes. Charming.

Luckily, he'd managed to leap over to my side of the table and prop me up.

Everyone was staring at me.

Arse-wrenchingly embarrassing.

Husband was requesting politely that the food be boxed to go.

I couldn't wait to get out of there, but as I moved to start gathering up my things, my coat and bag, I realized that my bum was wet.

Oh no.

For the love of all that's holy.

NO!

Yes indeed. Once again, my bladder buddy betrayed me, and yes, of course, I had just gulped down half a pint of water, which was now exiting swiftly by any means available. Mainly via the pants department. There was the imminent danger of drowning everyone in the restaurant in my own effluent unless I could escape speedy-like.

So that's what we did. I tried to wipe down the plastic banquette surreptitiously as I slid out, but a quick glance back revealed a giveaway Dibley-sized puddle under the table.

Obviously, I can never ever return to that restaurant. Unless, of course, I hand out anoraks and galoshes to everyone inside . . .

I clambered into the bath as soon as I could, had a good long sleep, and then I was easily well enough to drive the five hours home.

I still don't quite know what happened, but I've presumed I was just beyond tired.

An old, knackered showbiz twat.

And proud of it!

Ooo, I know I said this was the last of the piddle-related stories ... but I've just remembered something key that was also a bit widdly.

ELVIS'S DAUGHTERS

We did a *French and Saunders* sketch once where the fantastic Stephanie Beacham played an ex-lover of Elvis, the mother of twin daughters (us), his love children. The idea was that Elvis had once landed in Wolverhampton and we were the issue of their brief fling.

We were dressed as mini-Elvises, and although it was a silly, simple joke, just the nearness of Jennifer pulling an Elvis snarly face set me off and it was virtually impossible to get through the sketch without corpsing (laughing).

Fatty was just as bad.

You know that point where you are so lost in laughter that you have no control? It was that. In the end, the giggles themselves created more giggles and it was barely possible to continue. We did take after take that just collapsed. Stephanie found it amusing, I think, to begin with, but it honestly became ridiculously unprofessional. We simply COULD NOT get through it, and we could sense that the director, the crew and probably Stephanie herself were all running out of patience. It was no longer funny for them, which meant that the set became a bit tense – which in turn made it even funnier for us . . .

We behaved like naughty, irritating, selfish schoolgirls with a private joke. It was utterly unacceptable. Awful. Delicious.

We were in white Elvis-suits with rhinestones. Not the ideal outfit for a peeing misdemeanour.

But . . . hey.

You can't have *that* much fun without a certain amount of urinary indiscretion.

So, I obliged.

You're welcome.

Ooo, and there was one more moment, sorry.

I might as well own up to ALL of them.

We have a tour promoter we love called Paul Roberts, known to us as 'The General'. He's a cheerful, encouraging grafter who has accompanied us on pretty much every tour we've ever done.

He refers to us as 'The Dames' and has a regular joke where he asks, 'Are you decent?' when he knocks on the dressing room door after the show.

When we tell him we are, he always pretends to be disappointed that he's missed the chance to see us undressed and view the F&S baps up close.

'Damn,' he goes. Every time.

On the last night of our last show, he knocked on the door. 'Are you decent, Dames?'

'Yes!' we said, and so he came straight in to find us both topless, holding our bare tits for him to view.

The utter shock and, frankly, horror on his face was priceless. It was so good, I peed my pants.

I know.

HIPPO

In 2004, I received the phone call that pretty much every other British actor born after 1800 had already received . . .

Namely, to be in a *Harry Potter* film.

I was elated. I loved the whole *Harry Potter* shenanigans. We had read the books to our daughter, who was wide-eyed and eager to read herself thanks to those books, so I have a particular love of them because of that, and because of the genius of J. K. Rowling.

It doesn't happen often that I experience seething jealousy; I'm lucky that my green-eyed monster is pretty well caged up. I'm not saying it doesn't exist – it most certainly does – but it is under control MOST OF THE TIME.

I have witnessed many incidents in this 'business we call show' where folk have become eaten up with jealousy about parts they didn't get, or weren't considered for. It seems utterly ridiculous to take it personally when someone else is chosen instead of you. There are a zillion reasons why casting goes a certain way, but it takes some resilience to resist the idea that you personally have been found wanting.

It's key to remember that someone else's success IS NOT your failure.

I know this. I know it in my bones, and I don't usually experience jealousy. Much.

But...

I felt those irrational and stupid pangs when I watched the first *Harry Potter* films. Oh yes, I did.

I was busy brewing a nasty, putrid little pot of hot jealousy soup about ALL of the female roles that the many very-talented-indeed women had taken from me. Literally, from me. Even though I hadn't even auditioned. Helena Bonham Carter, Julie Walters (again), Emma Thompson, Imelda Staunton, Miriam Margolyes, you name it, I felt equally murderous about all of them. It didn't help that they were all fantastically good in their roles. That just added pus to the canker. Damn them all to hell. The hell where I'm in charge of the torture and, believe me, some of those tortures would involve dangling an Oreo cookie just out of reach of a tied-up *Harry Potter* actress. Yes. Serious hell, with major hurty stuff involved.

I confess all this so that you understand just how delighted I was to be asked. I was GAGGING FOR IT.

I had a little bit of a reality check when they delicately explained that the character they wanted me to play didn't have an actual name; she was simply called 'The Fat Lady'.

Yep. That helped to dilute any special and precious vibe I might've been experiencing for a hot five minutes. Not so special and precious now.

But hey . . .

Who cares . . . ?

I'm gonna be in a film with Robbie Coltrane and Alan Rickman and Maggie Smith and Michael Gambon and . . . and . . . oh dear . . . and Daniel Radcliffe, Rupert Grint and Emma Watson . . . who Fatty Saunders and I had just taken the right royal piss out of for Comic Relief.

Ah. Right. Yes.

I had just played a VERY bosomy Daniel Radcliffe and we'd had the best time poking fun at pretty much every concept and character in the franchise, including J. K. herself.

This was major karma right there.

So – I go for a meeting with the director, and en route I walk through the make-up room where, lo and behold, our three young leads are preparing for a scene.

If you look up the word 'toady' online, you might see a re-enactment of that little encounter. In an attempt to assuage any hatred these teenagers might have had for me, I put on a magnificent display of sycophantic, creepy grovelling of such ick that Uriah Heep would be proud.

Oh, they are marvellous.

Oh, they are clever.

Oh, they are talented.

Oh . . . shut up, French!

After sufficiently crawling up their bums, I make my way to the room where the director, Alfonso Cuarón, is. What an absolute peach of a chap he is. A Mexican director who made the beautiful film *Y Tu Mamá También*, who just happens to be funny and engaging and, coincidentally, as hot as a hot spicy thing. Nice. We have a successful meeting, we agree about everything to do with the character and I'm just about to leave, when he says:

Alfonso – You're fine with animals, yes?

Me – Yes, I love animals. Why?

Alfonso – Good, because there's a scene with a hippo.

And he closes the door, smiling.

Right. Okey doke.

A hippo. What? You mean a real hippo? An actual hippo? A hippo hippo?

So – the day comes for the filming, and it IS only one day. I'm only on this film for ONE SINGLE DAY.

In the morning, we shoot the scene where I am the portal to the Gryffindor common room. It's against a green screen (CGI), so I'm not involved with any other actors. We get this scene done pretty quickly, and all is well.

Now, it's time to shoot the scene with the hippo.

This is all at Leavesden Studios, which is comprised mainly of great big old air hangars. They take me into one of these huge hangars and directly into a pen with sawdust on the floor and ask me to stand in the very middle.

Enter the animal wrangler.

Now, I have had many dealings with such folk in my life. So much so that Fatty and I invented the characters Dot and May of Prickly Pear Farm, whose job it was to train animals for TV and films. Obviously, there are many different types of animal trainers, but all I will say is that SOME of them are challenging to warm to . . .

I can't remember the name of this particular bloke on *Harry Potter*, but I'm going to call him Colin.

Because he was a right Colin.

It's his job to brief me before they bring the hippo in. He has the air of a Marine briefing soldiers going into Vietnam. It's very, very serious. No room for levity.

Colin (semi-shouting) – Right. I'm in charge of this set now, so all eyes on me. Roger that? There is an actual living creature coming in here, so we need hush and concentration from you. Do you understand?

Me – Yes, Colin, I understand.

Colin – And whatever happens – you do NOT run. Do you understand?

Me – Yes, Colin, I understand.

Colin – Right. Listen up. Three key points incoming. Number One! This scene calls for a female hippo, but our cast member today is a male hippo. Do you understand?

Me – Yes, Colin, I understand.

Colin – Number Two! This hippo will, undoubtedly, attempt to sniff your privates. You do NOT run. Do you understand?

Me (faltering a bit) – Yes, Colin, I understand.

Colin – Number Three! And most importantly – the hippo MAY want to mate with you. If he does, his skin will foam slightly. You need to be alert to that and inform me IMMEDIATELY. You do NOT run. Do you understand?

Me (gulping heavily) – Umm . . . Yes, Colin, I understand.

With that, he goes off to get the hippo, leaving me terrified. It is quickly dawning on me that a hippo is, after all, a fairly mighty beast, a brute that should rightly be thumping about in the savannah, not filming in a hangar in Leavesden . . . where it can charge at a fat lady and trample her to a certain mushy death. A death from which she may not recover.

They back a horse-box-type trailer into the hangar and I can hear the monster snorting away inside.

I'm not ashamed to admit that a small amount of feminine wee (More pee? Do I ever stop leaking?) does trickle down my leg. I am petrified.

My heart is beating fast, my palms are sweaty and I start to shake a bit. I decide in that moment that I hate animals, actually. I hate all God's creatures, especially this bleddy great prehistoric bald beast that is going to surely kill me.

Colin opens up the back of the trailer, pulls down the ramp and goes in to bring out the colossus.

There's some beefy banging about, pounding and thudding.

I'm tempted to scarper.

Thump thump thump. Snort snort snort.

And then . . . here they come . . . they hove into view, and the creature that Colin is leading down the ramp is indeed a hippo, but it's the size of a Labrador.

Right.

The word absolutely NO ONE has used in reference to this hippo is:

PYGMY

This is a pygmy hippo.

Like a hippo that's shrunk in the wash.

Don't get me wrong, I'm still being heroically brave standing there. I'm not running.

I'm doing as directed.

I mean, it could still charge me, and it would be a hefty thwack to the knees . . . but I would likely survive.

Colin leads the dog-hippo to me.

And immediately, it does indeed sniff my privates. Awkward.

All the while, I'm thinking: 'Please God, don't let it smell the wee . . . don't let it mistake it for foreplay. Ugh.'

We do the little scene, which requires me to

'HIDE BEHIND THE HIPPO'.

When I initially read this direction in the script, I was obviously imagining a full-sized beast. In order to make this work, I have to crouch down behind it on all fours and try to pop up to make it seem big.

The scene is over in a matter of minutes, with no untoward incidents taking place.

It's over.

It's done.

Colin leads the hippo back to the trailer.

I'm left in the pen, with an abiding feeling of shame

      and regret

      and disappointment.

Why?

Because throughout the entire ordeal, that hippo's skin didn't foam once.

Yep.

I have failed to ignite the ardour of a pygmy hippo . . .

And what's even more troubling . . .

I cared.

What a twat.

DANGEROUS, STUPID STUFF

KNEE

I've already referred to the *Dibley* puddle jump. I can't deny that jumping into that puddle remains one of the most enjoyable moments of my work life. I can't take any credit for it; it was the idea of Richard Curtis and Paul Mayhew-Archer, who co-wrote *The Vicar of Dibley*.

Somehow this clip has crept into the annals of comedy consciousness, and it turns up again and again (which is good – I think I get 12p a go ... so watch me build a golden palace, and weep, folks). Ever since it was aired, over two hundred years ago, people have been reproducing the moment in one form or another.

I am sent endless GIFs (?), memes (?!) and reels (I'm using this terminology as if I have a clue what it all means – I don't) of various folk jumping into muddy puddles.

Someone's granny.

Their grandson.

Their grandson's puppy.

Their postman.

Their postman's puppy.

The strange bloke who lives in that house over the park.

His puppy.

Their mum.

And both her puppies.

(Talking of which, next time you see this clip, please notice that my giant bosoms jump into the puddle in a completely different time zone to me. It's about an hour behind, where they live.)

I'm fully aware that I am ALWAYS going to be associated, my whole life, with jumping into deep puddles, and that's honestly fine with me. The memories are nothing but happy.

But . . .

Being linked constantly with that puddle has brought some idiocy to my door.

Do you remember when darlin' Paul O'Grady used to have his own teatime chat show? It was very good and the viewing figures were high, so he managed to land plenty of top-quality guests. There was an occasion when he had to go off and do something famous and important and the producers asked me if I would step in as the host for one show. This was proper exciting, especially because the guests that were booked included the great Whoopi Goldberg, a woman I utterly adore. Of course, I said yes immediately.

In a giddy swirl, I said yes to EVERYTHING they asked me to do on that day, including the catastrophically misguided request to jump in a puddle to end the show.

What?

This was a TV studio, with a flat concrete floor. How on earth were they proposing to pull it off?

Some sadistic monster on the production side came up with the idea of constructing a twelve-foot-high hill out of scaffolding and covering it in AstroTurf, so that I would have a long enough drop to disappear into.

It was a big hollow tower, in effect, with nowhere for a huge tube of water to go. The evil assistant to the sadistic monster came up with a solution: they decided to make the entrance to the puddle out of silicone, a sort of shallow plastic valve with a membrane that would hold two inches of water above it, which would appear to all intents and purposes like a deep puddle. It would splash the water up as I jumped through it, apparently, and complete the illusion.

So, really, I was jumping into and through, a giant fake vulva . . .

SCREENS, PLEASE, DOCTOR FREUD, I'M JUMPING BACK INTO MY MOTHER'S WOMB!

'But Dawn,' you're asking, 'if there was no actual water, what exactly were you jumping into and on to?'

Thank you for asking, and it's a reasonable question. Perhaps one I also should've asked with a tad more circumspection at the time?

The floor manager took me around the back to see the full extent of this feat of bad engineering.

There was basically a twelve-foot drop on to a couple of thin crash mats on the floor.

Any fool would know that this was a disaster in the making.

Any fool but me.

Because I'm a twat.

The worst kind of twat at this point too. A defiant, would-be plucky, over-confident, self-assured twat.

The producers actually showed me the dangers, for heaven's sake. They were chewing their cheeks with anxiety, checking I was all right with this set-up of the twelve-foot fall on to crash mats? The ball was entirely in my court.

So, I'm thinking, well, it's a challenge.

And I'm British.

And I have an older brother who taught me when I was very little that if you refuse a challenge, you will forever be labelled 'a girl'.

So – I am British.

I am NOT 'a girl'.

So, of course, I'm going to do the jump.

However stupid.

The show went well. John Barrowman was on and he was being camp and generous. There were some silly games. Whoopi was a total dream, and so we came to the end of the show . . .

Much against their better judgement, both John and Whoopi joined me at the top of the precarious 'hill' to witness the jump. Whoopi, especially, looked terrified on my behalf and, perversely, her fear for me doubled up my determination to prove that this was going to be a piece of piss.

I smile and jump, straight through the plastic vulva. In for a penny, in for a pound or a million. I land very heavily and awkwardly twelve feet below on the mats, with my left leg twisted under me like a pretzel. I've heard the worst twanging noise imaginable, and I know I'm in trouble.

But I'm British.

And I'm not a girl.

So, I'm going to complete this sketch if it kills me, which it very nearly has.

I climb up the ladder placed next to me, and I poke my head out through the puddle fanny to finish the joke off and end the show.

TA DA!

I'm in agony, something is very wrong, but I hear the end credits music so I smile and wave. Doctor Showbiz is in town.

The audience and the guests go home.

I'm back on the studio floor, saying goodbye to the production folk. I'm hobbling quite badly by this time. They're offering me doctors and splints and air ambulances, but I'm full of dismissive bluster.

Me – Nah, no need, ta. It's all fuss and nonsense, honestly. I'm absolutely fine. Leg is a bit gippy, that's all. Absolutely fine. Bye!

I climb into my car and drive home to Cornwall, and all the way I'm trying to convince myself that everything is all right.

It wasn't.

For eighteen months or so after that, I had to resort to walking with a stick quite regularly.

Cut to:

About seven years ago, it really started to hurt badly again. It felt like bone-on-bone crunching. Ow. It was time to surrender and I went to see a knee surgeon, a bloke called Simon Ball, a brilliant chap who works with lots of sports people. He did various X-rays and scans and manipulated it a bit to assess the situation.

We sat down for the consultation:

Simon – OK. Well, your legs are quite strong, actually.

Me (attempting pathetic levity) – Thanks. You're not so bad yerself.

Simon – Out of interest, have you ever had a trauma to that knee?

Me – You could say so, yeah, I jumped into a puddle fanny for a laugh.

Simon looks at me blankly. He has no idea what the dick I'm talking about. Neither do I. Shut up, French.

Simon – You have severe osteoarthritis in there, and there's lots of inflammation. I'm going to tell you that you seriously need to rest it for six weeks or so … but I suspect that, like ALL ELITE ATHLETES …

Me – Whoa there! Wait one pickin' cotton moment, Mister knee doctor man. Shush a minute. Look, I know you are going to finish that sentence with something disappointing, but would you mind indulging me for a second or two, just hold that thought there. No one has ever before, or will ever again, described me in those terms, so just let me relish this unique moment, please. Yes. According to you – a man of experience and extensive medical learning – I, Dawn Roma Twat French, am AN ELITE ATHLETE … and … wait a minute … and savour it, and savour it ……… and, OK, doc, carry on now, please.

Simon – As I was going to say, like ALL ELITE ATHLETES, you're gonna tell me you're going back on stage tonight, just like they tell me they're going to play on Centre Court at Wimbledon, or at Wembley, or at The Oval, at Twickenham, or wherever, yes?

Me – Yes. Correct.

Simon – So, I'm going to give you a temporary fix, which is an injection directly into the knee with a steroid and a lubricant but, Dawn, this is only a temporary measure. Eventually, you are going to need a knee replacement operation. In the meantime, you can only have THREE of these injections . . .

And he blethered on about the possible side effects, etc.

Me – OK, well – I need the first one right now, please. Immediately. Soon. Now. Thank you.

So, he gave me the first injection that very day and honestly, it was magical. I'd hobbled into that guy's office, and I ran and jumped and skipped out of it and went on stage that night and finished my tour with little to no pain. It was miraculous.

Lovely.

I had complete pain relief for about three months or so, until it started to slowly wear off and the grinding ache began to return.

I was hyper-aware that I only had TWO more of these wondrous injections left before the big op. I knew I needed to eke them out, be sparing, only use them when I had big physical jobs to do at work.

So, in between those jobs, I settled for hobbling about and necking plenty of pain relief, not something I felt particularly comfortable with. Not that I was at the Elvis/toilet end of the spectrum, but I'd only ever taken one or two Nurofen occasionally prior to this, so I felt a bit like I was starting some kind of filthy, dangerous habit.

Along came the offer of a panto at the Palladium, the first ever that I was tempted to do. I knew it would be physically gruelling.

Out of interest, the Palladium was built as a variety theatre, so has very little room in the wings and the stage isn't very deep. This meant that once we had all our huge props installed – dragons, giants, etc., there was no way to travel across the stage once the show started. We always had to go downstairs, stage left, under the stage behind the orchestra pit and up the steep stairs on the other side, stage right. Lots of steps – not great for bad knees. As you travel under the stage, you pass a wall that has various plaques on it, citing many wonderful performers whose careers flourished there, including the fabulous Bruce Forsyth, whose ashes are interred there. Of course, every time I passed that, every night without fail, I'd nod to him and say, 'Nice to see you . . .'

SIDEBAR

Taking this panto job was the cue to have the second, precious injection.

Marvellous. Miraculous. Thank you.

I completed that run relatively pain-free with the help of some judicious strapping, but then, of course, it gradually wore off and I was aware that I only had ONE more pop.

I went for more than a year grunting in pain and dragging my crumbly ol' left knee about. I walked less because it hurt to do so. I became much more sedentary than it made me happy to be.

Along came a lovely job called *The Trouble with Maggie Cole*, a comedy-drama I'd developed with my friend, comedy producer and all-round babe, Sophie Clarke-Jervoise. This was another physical job that required me to have working legs.

I had the THIRD, and final, injection.

I knew I was nearing the inevitable, but the thought of the op made me shudder, so, of course, when that last injection wore off, I limped my way through life in a big vat of denial and bluster for ages. Ow.

Then . . .

Along came *Death on the Nile*.

What a fantastic opportunity.

But . . .

It was a period piece, and that meant HEELS and long days of standing.

It wasn't long before I was in terrible trouble.

None of the painkillers touched the sides. Or the front. Or the back. Or anywhere.

I booked a crisis meeting with Simon.

He met me very early in the morning, before filming started that day.

I was using the stick to walk, and I was on the edge of tears.

Me – Right. The time has come . . . I need to book the surgery NOW, as soon as this film finishes shooting.

Simon – Right. Just to clarify. Why do you want the surgery now?

Me – Because the pain is unbearable. Please and thank you.

Simon – Right. I see. But the injections are still effective?

Me – Yes! But I can't have any more, can I?!

Simon – Right. Why?

Me (barely controlling myself) – Because you said I can only have THREE! I've had THREE!

Simon – Dawn. Oh, Dawn. Three. A. Year . . .

SILENCE AS GIANT PENNY DROPS AND I REALIZE I HAVE
BEEN SUFFERING FOR MANY YEARS FOR NO REASON ...

AAAAAAGH!

Me – Oh. My. Actual. God. You mean to tell me I could've had
three a year all this time?

Simon – Yes. That's what I told you.

And right there, ladles and jellyspoons, is why you should always
write down instructions that doctors give you, rather than relying on
your stupid, old, fuddled brain to remember key details.

Why didn't I listen properly?!

Yes, you know why.

Because I'm a massive TWAT!

That is why.

Ridiculous.

Update: as I write this book, after several more years of relatively successful injections, I genuinely have come to the end of their efficacy and the surgery is finally booked in for just before Christmas.

Hurray!

ALMERÍA

We made a film for the Comic Strip called *A Fistful of Travellers' Cheques* in 1984, I think. It's a Spaghetti Western parody in which Rik Mayall and Pete Richardson play two friends, Carlos and Miguel, who are obsessed with roleplay, and try to live out their Lee Van Cleef fantasies.

The decision was made to shoot it in the home of the Spaghetti Western, Almería in Spain, which has small towns and desert and beach all within spitting distance of each other, so perfect for all the settings we needed.

These were still the very early days of Comic Strip filming and I could not quite believe that we were all flying out to Spain to dress up and show off with our chums – that this was my actual job now.

The characters that Fatty and I were playing were a couple of Aussie backpackers driving about in a VW campervan, called Jackie and Shona. Our parts were fairly minor in the film, so when we arrived in Almería, we had a few days off before we were called to shoot any scenes.

This was fantastic news. We spent time at the beach and exploring all the local tabernas until getting together with the rest of the cast and crew in the evenings. It genuinely felt like halcyon days, the best kind of holiday. Not like work whatsoever. Carefree.

We were sharing a little villa with two bedrooms. Fatty and her then-boyfriend in one room and me solo in the other. We slept in as long as we could on those precious days off.

About five days in, we were finally called to set. The call sheet informed us that a car would pick the two of us up at 6 a.m. It was my job to be the alarm. I set mine for 5.30. I duly woke up and, in an effort not to fall back to sleep immediately, I attempted to sit up.

What happened next was very odd.

It was as if I'd been thwacked in the face with a frying pan in a *Tom and Jerry* cartoon.

I immediately fell backwards on to my pillow. My head was a balloon full of cement, too heavy to lift up. Eventually, I managed to roll sideways off my bed and on to the floor. I was groggy and confused. I crawled to the door, opened it, and shouted to Jennifer. She mumbled something and then I heard a thud. Her door opened and there she was, also crawling on the floor. We quickly realized that all three of us were in big trouble. None of us could stand up, so we crawled to the front door and outside.

It later transpired that we were being stealthily poisoned by a carbon monoxide leak from a faulty boiler. A silent, odourless, ninja killer that came for us in the night.

I'm pretty sure that, if we hadn't had that early morning call, we wouldn't be here now because we wouldn't have attempted to wake up and the gas would've finished us off.

Now, there isn't really a culpable twat in this story, save possibly the landlord, but it stays with me when I remember scary Comic Strip incidents.

CLIFF

During the filming of *South Atlantic Raiders*, another Comic Strip film we made in 1990, there was a scene that required me to be hanging off a cliff. We filmed in Devon, as we so often did. I had mistakenly believed that this would be some kind of stunt person or even a dummy hanging from a rope harness ... or something ... but no.

Before I could even think about it, I'd agreed (death wish?) to be hung off the cliff with the sea crashing below. I remember looking at the man who was also harnessed on to be the sort of ballast/counterweight to me, the 'safety' person. He was easily in his sixties and about half my considerable weight. On reflection, I reckon they just asked the guy from the ice-cream van in the car park ...

Somehow, I didn't die.

BIKE

When we were filming *The Famous Five* films, and the four of us were cycling around the lanes on old-fashioned sit-up bikes, mine had a crossbar because my character George was a qualified tomboy. If you're a short woman, a big bike with a high crossbar is your enemy. Not just an enemy, actually, it is also your assailant. It is, quite frankly, prepared to penetrate you without your permission, at any given moment, when you need to come to a stop. It wants to father your kids.

I was terrified of that bike and had several awful moments with it.

One was when we were due to ride downhill in a field that was quite rough. The brakes had always been dodgy, but just prior to this shot I was aware that they had entirely broken. We didn't have much time to get the shot – we needed the light – and so, for some cretinous reason, I agreed to do it anyway, knowing that the only way to get off the bike at the bottom of the hill was to hurl myself from it before we hit the inevitable hedge at the end. I attempted this utterly misguided feat unsuccessfully. Suffice to say that the bike and I consummated our relationship.

I am now the mother of three small trikes.

--- ✳ ---

Another bike incident occurred when we did a scene that involved a big American Cadillac driving very fast (containing baddies, of course) through the middle of the Famous Five, who would part to allow it. It was easy for the others to stand aside because their bikes were their friends. Mine was not. I couldn't get out of the way quickly enough, so the car actually ploughed into me, at speed, and I was hurled to the side.

It was shocking and very painful.

What did I do?

Immediately jumped up and, with hot embarrassment coursing through my British veins, declared: 'I'm fine! No prob. It was just a car knocking me over. All good. Fine.'

Honestly.

Crown me Queen of Twatville.

LULU

We decided to do a Tarantino parody in *French and Saunders*. We chose *Pulp Fiction*, and we set it in our White Room, the 'home' of F&S, if you like.

The whole idea was that we'd taken Lulu, the actual living legend Lulu, hostage. Every time she attempted to sing her big hit 'Shout', we threatened to shoot her to smithereens if she did it again.

Jennifer was John Travolta, natch.

I was Samuel L. Jackson, of course.

We did our best to emulate their famous scene in the movie but, on top, we threw in a few typical F&S gags – pretending to also be Robson & Jerome, for instance. All silly stuff. Somehow, we had more freedom to be surreal if we were in the White Room, rather than re-creating a movie shot for shot. We were able to inject a bit more low-level F&S stupidity – always my favourite thing.

So, there we are.

The White Room set.

White sofa.

Lulu sitting on that sofa in a white blouse.

In order to achieve the carnage we need it to be, the set and Lulu have to be properly rigged with various blood-spurting devices. There are tubes in the walls and in the sofa, all primed to pump the 'blood' when we eventually 'shoot' her.

Lulu has squibs placed strategically all over her upper body. Squibs are like little balloons or condoms with exploding pellets in them with the fake blood. She has a breast-plate under her blouse to protect her – they ARE explosives, after all.

The special effects (SFX) guys carefully talk her through the whole thing, explaining that so long as she follows their instructions to the letter, she'll be perfectly safe.

She DOES have a couple of squibs placed on the inner crease of her elbows, so they explain that when the moment comes, she needs to throw her arms OUTWARDS, rather than pull them in around and across her body. This way, the squibs will be free to explode.

Lulu agrees to all of this.

Why?

Because she's a GODDESS, that's why!

So, the moment comes when we shoot this bloodbath scene. We have to pre-record it the night before we do the show live in front of the audience because the scene is too tricky to do live. The plan is to re-do the whole scene the following night but slip in this pre-recorded bit so the live audience gets to see the WHOLE sketch.

So.

It's about 8 p.m. on a Saturday night at the old BBC recording studios at White City.

Lulu is covered in explosives.

What on earth could go wrong . . . ?!

We are recording this bit last because it will be messy and is impossible to repeat. We need to get it right – Lulu in the White Room in a bloodbath.

All eyes are on Lulu.

The director calls for hush and instructs, 'ACTION!'

We fake-shoot her with our fake machine guns. Blam. Blam. Blam.

She writhes around on the white sofa as all the squibs and effects go off all over and around her.

There is 'blood' everywhere.

Up the walls, all over the sofa, all over Lulu, whose white blouse is dripping with claretty goo.

There is a moment of silence.

Then – we all break out into huge applause.

It has gone well; it all looks suitably horrific.

Lulu sits up from her après murder slouch.

She is laughing. She's buzzing.

It's been a huge thrill and it's worked!

Then.

Lulu says (in a Scottish accent. Because she is Scottish), 'Oh, ow. It's hurting a bit here.'

She points to the crease in her elbow.

We can all see what's happened.

In the madness of the moment, she did indeed pull her arms across her chest, one of the squibs has exploded into her skin and she's bleeding quite profusely. It's hard to distinguish her real blood from the sopping fake blood covering her entire torso.

We have to send for medical help.

But.

This is the old, old, old BBC studios.

At 8 p.m.

On a Saturday night.

Where 'medical help' appears to be a Rip Van Winkle of a bloke in a cupboard under the stairs, who has a Fisher Price first-aid kit with three Mutant Ninja Turtle plasters in it and a tube of Bonjela.

There's a phone next to him.

He's napping with a cheeky fag stuck to his lip.

That phone hasn't rung for twenty years.

It rings.

He jumps.

Rip Van Winkle – Hello? I see. An incident in studio 2B. Right. I'm on my way . . .

He picks up his tiny kit and saunters to the studio. No urgency. He wants to finish his fag en route. Shame to waste it.

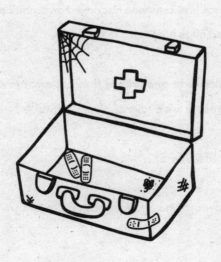

When he arrives at the studio – he opens the door to a harrowing, grisly scene.

A total massacre has happened, apparently.

It is a bloodbath, a slaughter with a seemingly dead Lulu at the centre of it, and he's only got three plasters.

He starts to wobble.

He is going to faint.

Luckily, meanwhile, someone has called an ambulance, and Lulu is loaded in and off to hospital.

She has a skin graft and returns the next night to complete the sketch in front of the live audience.

What a total TROOPER!

So – we, as French and Saunders, can claim that we have indeed shot Lulu.

In every sense of the word.

THE ANASTACIA MOMENT

This is quite possibly my most twatty incident, because it affected other people in the long run . . .

As I write this, I'm not entirely sure I properly understand exactly what happened, but I ask you to indulge me as I attempt to unpick it. Maybe then, it will make more sense.

Here goes . . .

It was the final series of *French and Saunders*, which had, in many ways, been my favourite. We decided to write it very much centred around our actual (but heightened) experience of creating the series, so there were plenty of scenes set in our fictional office at the BBC with Liza Tarbuck playing our extremely frustrated producer and Maggie Steed playing our extremely frustrated agent, Maureen (with alarming accuracy). Fatty and I were completely at home playing monster versions of ourselves, lazy and grumpy (perfect name for a double act like us, on reflection!). Being 'behind the scenes', so to speak, opened up a whole raft of new self-referential and self-deprecating jokes.

I will not easily forget the joy of playing with Fatty, on that series. And always actually, but for some reason, especially on THAT series. I have such fond memories, for instance, of a scene where we practised curtseying, because in real life, Jennifer was going to some Royal do at the Palace where she was going to meet the Queen, and we had actually discussed this at great length while we were writing. It was only the slightest of tips sideways to turn that silly conversation into a five-minute slice of puerile joy in the show. It was the closest we'd ever been to our authentic selves, and something about sending up the worst parts of our real selves was especially joyful.

Interspersed with the backstage bits, we also did some filming and TV parodies, of course, but the line between backstage and front of camera was fine.

One such sketch took place in the toilets at the BBC. It was a conceit we'd discussed many times and had become a bit of a private running joke – namely the idea that certain iconic singers we adored, Madonna, Celine Dion, etc., could easily be replaced by us at the drop of a hat should there be a medical emergency, etc. (I know). Jennifer and I both grew up pretending to be various pop stars in front of our bedroom mirrors, wielding hairbrushes as microphones, just like everyone else. For us, however, this childhood fantasy had simply morphed into an adult fantasy and sometimes even into our actual job. Unlike most folk, we were permitted and indeed PAID to do said pretending. We have spent our adult life in the literal and metaphorical dressing-up box.

So, we had shared the fantasy that, whilst sitting in our cars, we'd both enjoyed singing along at the top of our voices, and imagining the moment when we have to step on to the stage at the Royal Albert Hall or wherever, to stand in for . . . Beyoncé or P!nk . . . or whoever we had a crush on at the time.

We decided to work this idea into the show and when we discovered Anastacia was in town, she was the PERFECT person for it. I adored her song 'I'm Outta Love' and so we begged her to be in the sketch with us, and like the dreamboat she is, she agreed.

The idea being, that she would come into the loos whilst I was still in the cubicle, and she would overhear me singing her song and owing to my utter brilliance (!) she would instantly invite me to join her onstage at *Top of the Pops* to sing with her.

The delicious coincidence was that *Top of the Pops* were actually shooting in the next-door studio, and they agreed to let Anastacia and me hijack their stage for a few minutes to do our duet as the punchline to the sketch. The audience was THEIR audience, the cameras and production were THEIRS; we were basically invading their space.

All of that was tickety-boo.

I think where it went wrong for me was when I tried on my costume. I'd told our lovely costume designer, Rebecca Hale (who we'd worked with for years, still do) that I wanted her to copy Anastacia's updated cowgirl look. Remember when Madonna was sporting that same look? Gingham and denim and cowboy boots and big belts and Stetson hats – but put together in an edgy, fashion-y way? That's what I was after.

Now, look, admittedly this was going to be a stretch. I was nearly twenty-one stone at that time. The biggest I'd ever been (I have all kinds of theories about that but it's a whole other book, I reckon!). I was never going to look slick like them. I accept that. I've spent forty years being considerably bigger physically than any of the people we take the mickey out of; it doesn't faze me. In fact, it's an essential part of the delight of a parody joke, and it's a key part I'm collaborating on at all times. I'm complicit in the gag.

But.

On this occasion, I put the outfit on ... and ... it was seriously awful and twenty thousand kinds of wrong. Nothing about it hit the mark of being anything like Anastacia. NOTHING. It was so spectacularly wide of the mark as to be pretty offensive. I couldn't believe that I was going to face Anastacia looking that bad, when she knew that the point of the joke was that I was attempting to emulate her.

Instead, I was immolating her. Savagely slaughtering her image. Right in front of her, and in front of an actual living *Top of the Pops* audience.

The moment I put the dreadful, inaccurate, insulting outfit on, Rebecca couldn't help herself, she literally fell on her back on the floor of my dressing room like an upturned tortoise, and she howled with laughter. She couldn't breathe.

In one way, I understood, I was a frightful sight. EVERYTHING about it was a violation. I looked like someone's rather sad and dopey sister, born out of a hideous incestuous sibling relationship in Redneck country, who has taken up line dancing as part of a rehabilitation programme. I had a huge tan skirt and tassels and a man's shirt and a waistcoat ... and the cowboy boots didn't fit over my calves, so we settled for some inappropriate mumsy slingbacks.

WHAAAT THE FUH . . . ?!?!

And my tightless mottled-white stumpy legs were in full view.

I'd genuinely never felt so ugly.

This is important.

I'd often voluntarily, happily been 'ugly' for HUNDREDS of sketches. I've never minded what something looks like, so long as it's servicing the joke right.

The mirror was clearly telling me why this was so painfully abhorrent.

Because the joke was ON me. I was suddenly entirely out of control of it, and it was too late to rectify it.

The first part of the sketch, in the loos, had gone well, but now we had to film this second, performance part.

God bless Anastacia. I fully expected her to strike me when she first saw me. Rebecca followed me into the *Top of the Pops* studio, but she was still struggling to suppress her hilarity. She was crying as she attempted to mute her reaction, as Anastacia inspected me up and down. What the hell was going through her mind?

'Is this what these crazy chicks think I look like? Book me into the Betty Ford Clinic IMMEDIATELY.'

(I remember Darcey Bussell similarly examining me when I did a mirror routine with her. I looked pretty awful then too, but I completely controlled that moment, that costume and I LOVED it all. It's honestly not about the look. Well, not only.)

I apologized profusely to Anastacia, as I could see she was perplexed. If you are a guest on a show like ours, you have to totally trust the folk you're working with. It's their show, their joke.

I felt we'd let her down.

But of course, we went ahead and shot it.

I looked out at the sea of confused faces amongst the vast *Top of the Pops* audience. They seriously were having problems processing just exactly what they were looking at. I understood. So was I. What was going on?

If I, the perpetrator of the gag, didn't fully invest in it or understand it, how are the audience supposed to?

All I had to do was sing along (badly) beside her.

I did that.

A couple of times.

She was so generous and encouraging.

Anastacia – It's really funny.

Me – Ha ha, yeah, thanks, is it? OK.

I was dying inside.

It took about forty minutes to shoot.

It felt like forty years.

I couldn't wait for it to be over.

When it was, I thanked her,

I thanked the crew,

I said goodnight to everyone.

I climbed into my car, and as I pulled away from the BBC in White City, I burst into hot, angry tears. I properly sobbed all the twenty-eight miles home. I couldn't quite fathom what I was feeling.

A big part of it was a kind of humiliation, I think, but I'm sure there must've been a cauldron of other, deeper, bubbly stuff cooking away underneath that temporary embarrassment.

I'm still perplexed.

But — the fact is that as I drove away that day, I resolved not to continue to make *French and Saunders*, the sketch show, any more. I meant it. I still mean it.

Don't get me wrong; of course, we'd still do the odd sketch for Comic Relief or whatever, and we'd still work together doing plenty of other things.

But —

The sketch show needed to be history.

I wanted to leave it, still enjoying it, and I'd had a little taste of not that. It was almost as if it was too lovely a part of my life to have spoilt in any way.

I don't believe it was just the Anastacia moment, I think that was a tipping point, but still . . . my decision would greatly affect Jennifer's life.

As always, when we did discuss it, albeit briefly (yes, the discussion took about two minutes), she wrapped her understanding around me, however baffling it might've been for her, and made it all right.

That's what people who love each other do. Make it all right. Even to be a twat.

So, it is.

I saw that sketch again recently and it's OK. Not too dreadful. Not as awful as my memory would have it.

I'm still left with some puzzlement about it all, even though I drove that particular decision bus.

Perhaps some things aren't supposed to make sense?

I don't regret it for a second though, and ALL of my F&S memories are fantastically intact.

Like a lovely big house we built together, where we once happily lived.

We've just moved to a bungalow, is all.

And it's by the sea.

BEING A BIT PRECIOUS AND SALTY

ANKLES

One of the films that we shot in the series *Murder Most Horrid* was called 'The Case of the Missing'. I played a policewoman, so the costume was a bit grim – bad skirt, black tights, flat shoes type of thing. Not a great look for me, it did no favours for my barrel of a body. (Skirts require waists. I've never owned one. A waist, I mean. I've definitely owned a skirt, I've attempted a skirt on several occasions, but the top of it always begins just below the bosoms and, sadly, the overall effect is the human embodiment of surrender and desolation, so I've given up with them.)

We were always up against it timewise with this series and so, occasionally, we would send a second, smaller unit of crew to pick up incidental shots that didn't require me to be there.

One such moment happened when the director decided he needed an extra shot of my character walking away near a canal. Since that shot was on my back, he decided to put my stand-in in the costume and shoot with her to save time. Nobody would know the difference, he assured me. It was only to be a walking shot, mainly on the legs, a bit like *The Bill* titles. The idea was to edit this shot in later and, of course, I didn't see it until the actual screening in front of the whole cast and crew, when it was all done and dusted.

So, my experience of seeing this was a bit traumatic (I'm exaggerating here, for sympathy).

I'm watching the film and it's all going swimmingly –

There's me driving a car.

There's me answering the phone.

There's me interrogating someone.

There's me walking along a canal . . .

HANG ON A MINUTE!

Whose legs are those? Whose back is that? Whose ankles are those?

There was a close-up on the ankles. With the greatest of respect to my darlin' stand-in, we have very different ankles. If we were to have a competition about who has the best physical features all-round, she would most certainly win, hands down . . .

But . . .

I have the better ankle.

Sorry to boast, but I just do.

My torso is a barrel, my feet are a hirsute abhorrence, my shins are trees . . .

But my ankles are rather well-turned. I've inherited them from my grandmother (it must've been painful to donate them). They're all I have that's even a tiny bit refined.

Yes, I have good ankles.

These were not my ankles and, in a fit of pathetic pique, I went into a full-on grump, begging the producer to edit out that shot. She quite rightly put me firmly in my place by pointing out that the film was now edited, graded and locked down, so that would be a giant unnecessary faff. I tried my best pouting. To no avail.

Of course, it's an utterly twattish thing to have any beef about. I was being extraordinarily puerile, but to this day, I'm (sorta) ashamed to say that if I ever see this little film, that moment is THE ONLY THING I can focus on.

Let it go, Frenchie!

And stop being a twat.

On the whole ankles thing – I ought to make something clear:

I used to have rather good ankles, yes. Literally on the DAY I turned sixty, something happened to my ankles where they swelled up pretty much overnight and have remained bloated ever since. So much so, that they are indiscriminate from my overly beefy calves. They are conjoined. It's an awful sight. I've renamed them 'cankles'. I've concluded that this phenomenon is either the natural order for the more mature lady

OR

I am being punished for being a twat about my ankles back then.

It's more likely the latter.

POOL

Oh Lord, I'm now remembering I had another idiotic, inexplicable and, frankly, unforgivable moment when we were shooting a drama series I loved very much, called *Delicious,* for Sky. The show was about four generations of women and their various and complicated relationships with one particular man, who dies (spoiler alert!) in the first episode. He is variously a husband, an ex, a father and a son to the women and they are left to deal with the detritus of his messy legacy.

Sheila Hancock played the mother.

I played the ex-wife.

Emilia Fox played the current wife.

Tanya Reynolds played the daughter.

And gorgeous Iain Glen played the man in question.

Anyhoo . . . we were shooting at a wonderful venue called Pentillie Castle in Cornwall and on this occasion, we were filming a night shot at a pool party. The pool itself wasn't very warm, but no matter, I didn't have to be in it. I had to sit on the side of it and do a semi-drunk, rather emotional scene with Emilia. We started the scene and, as with all filming, you have to do the same scene repeatedly, from many angles. Patience is what is required.

Not my strong suit but, in most cases, I don't have a problem. That's part of the job.

Although I was sitting on a mat to provide some buffer between my considerable arse and the cold of the concrete on the side of the pool, my feet were dangling in the cold water and I was starting to get chilly.

Now listen, when you are filming, there's an army of folk who are there to help, so the wardrobe department gave me blankets and hot-water bottles and hand-warmers and everything and everything . . . but, obviously, my toes had to remain in the cold water for continuity when we were actually 'turning'.

Something very strange came over me. I suddenly hated everything about the situation. The cold, the night, the place, the scene – all of it.

Sitting here now writing this, I look at the whole picture – I was filming something I loved with people I really like, in my own county, near my home, surrounded by beauty and happy, willing folk. There just WASN'T anything to moan about, frankly.

Yet . . .

I disappeared into a mystifying tunnel of bleakness that night. It was as if the cold night air froze all the blood and air inside me. My bones calcified and I just . . . sorta . . . stopped.

That had never happened to me before. I quietly imploded, detached and wasn't really there.

I didn't move. I put my head down, stayed shush, did the lines as and when I was asked, but was really just a useless lump of inert flesh sitting on the side of a pool. I knew it was happening, but I felt oddly unable to staunch the childish sulk, so I surrendered instead, and I'd never done that before.

I've not experienced it since.

I was a (sexless) *petit mort*, where I seemed to lose touch, temporarily, with my real conscious self, with my conscience. It was selfish.

Why didn't I just shake myself out of it?

On reflection, it seems like massively self-indulgent behaviour.

Either way, 'twat' is writ large over that memory for me.

Which is useful.

Because I don't want it to happen again.

Sometimes I think that is the very purpose of twatting – to learn from it and know how NOT to be in future.

THE MARK

On the subject of moments that were kept in films or TV that bother me, even though no one else would notice:

I made a film called *Tender Loving Care*, which was a BBC *Screen One* written by someone I truly love, the force of good that is Lucy Gannon. It was about a murdering nurse, someone who saw themselves as some sort of Angel of Mercy, who 'helped' old and lonely patients to slip away. It was a fairly gritty film and the first where I was playing straight. I was nervous, and the amazing Rosemary Leach helped to show me some acting ropes, for which I'm forever grateful.

In one shot, I needed to be watching her through a window. The director wanted two sizes on this shot, and it involved me taking a step forward during the shot. It was critical for the focus-puller on the camera that I hit my mark exactly. The mark was tape on the floor. I was new to this and I didn't know how else to do it accurately without looking down to find the mark. The director told me to go ahead and do that and, once in place, to resume the 'watching'. He said the journey to the mark would be edited out.

So – that's what I did:

ACTING. LOOKING. ACTING. LOOKING. BIT MENACING ...

DROP OUT OF CHARACTER. LOOK AT FLOOR.
STEP FORWARD ON TO MARK. SETTLE. LOOK UP.

RESUME 'ACTING'.

To my horror, ALL OF THIS was in the final edit. I thought it was howlingly obvious, but zero people noticed it. Eh?!

So much for 'acting'!

My nurse character murdered her patients by bringing them a 'special cocktail', which was essentially a mahoossive sedative, and then she would, in effect, drown them with water.

When my very badly behaved grandmother Lil, known to me as 'Evil Granny', was quite poorly in hospital in her late eighties, one night she beckoned me close and whispered in my ear, 'Bring me the special cocktail ...'

I knew what she was asking but, of course, I couldn't do that.

Instead, I answered her, 'I'll give you two hundred quid if you get better.'

Suffice it to say, she was out of hospital by the end of the week and lived for many more years!

BBC FRONT GATE

There was a time in the noughties when security at the BBC became ridiculously tight.

The guys (and it was ALWAYS guys) on the front gate at White City, where the studios are, turned into officious monsters.

Many was the time when they wouldn't let us in, even on days when we were due in the studio, or even when we were doing something live.

It was always humiliating:

Man – Yes?

Me – I'm here to record our show, *French and Saunders*.

Man – And you are?

Me – Dawn French.

Man – Don Tinch? Not on the list, sorry.

Me – No, DAWN FRENCH.

Man – Dan Trench?

Me – DAWN. FRENCH.

(Meanwhile, fans are shouting at me to sign things from behind the barrier they had there.)

Man – Nope. Not on the list.

Me – What shall I do?

Man – Up to you.

Me – Shall I go in and make the show we've written and planned for six months? Or shall I maybe just go home . . . ?

Man – As I say, Don – up to you.

Me – You seriously aren't going to let me in?

Man – Not on the list.

Me – What about if I show you my driver's licence? Is that enough proof?

Man – Doesn't mean anything. Not on the list.

Me – How can I prove who I am or what I do?

Man – No idea.

Me (losing it) – WOULD YOU LIKE TO TAKE A SWAB? INSIDE OF THE MOUTH, FOR DNA? OR PERHAPS YOU'D LIKE TO DO A CERVICAL SMEAR . . . ?

Man – Uncalled for.

Me (desperate now) – Right. Sorry. Yes. Would it help if I told you . . . (whispers something so fans don't hear the ignominy of it all).

Man – Can't hear you.

Me – (slightly louder whisper)

Man – Nope. Still can't hear you.

Me (shouting) – I'M LENNY HENRY'S WIFE!!

Man – Ah. Right, well in that case, in you go, madam.

He raises the barrier.

I MEAN.

Honestly.

TWATS. Both of us.

AWARDS

OK, it's a sticky ol' subject.

And it's properly a fine line between standing firmly in my truth, and being a mammoth twat, I know that.

I have NEVER felt comfortable about awards for the arts.

At least, not the competition-style awards.

I quite like the 'well done for being good at stuff and still being alive'-type of awards, which you might get for a body of work, say.

I don't like it when ANYONE in the creative industries is up against another, be it actor, comedian, writer, producer, singer, musician or ANY kind of artist. It seems to me that there ISN'T a person who can judge this, never mind whole panels of folk.

How can there be a winner out of five unbelievably good performances as a lead actor in five very different plays? THEY ARE SIMPLY NOT COMPARABLE.

If you sell cars, it's easy to reward the person who sold the most (although I bet there are mitigating factors with even that). It is, at least, a fact. That person sold a hundred, this person sold seventy. So that person is the winner. Have a prize.

Art isn't like that.

Sorry (not sorry) if that sounds precious, but it's true. It is impossible to choose a winner, in my opinion.

I wish we didn't do it.

However, I acknowledge, of course, that these big, lavish ceremonies are a business in themselves and I guess they bring attention to the various departments within the biz of show. That, in itself, means it's all open to a million corruptions.

We know that Hollywood gets behind certain films. There is marketing ringfenced for exactly that purpose, so the manipulation of a supposedly level-playing-field competition is blatant.

We all buy into it.

I know that.

When I was in my twenties, I went to various award ceremonies with Len, who was nominated a few times, but pretty much always missed out to other people. Even when, later on, he did sometimes win, it all felt ridiculous to me. I witnessed that the high you get from being chosen, followed by the low from losing, is nowt less than schizophrenic in its polarity. It's quite cruel in a way.

And yet, you're expected to just suck it up.

Repeatedly. Y'know, 'that's showbiz' . . .

The whole industry is full enough of rejection without this farcical coconut shy of a sham. I also think that our business gives us rewards enough in attention and dosh. We are largely a group of individuals who very often struggle with issues of self-esteem and the need for acknowledgement, it's a bit of a sickness really, so it seems doubly vicious to set up these showy coliseums in which all ends of this grisly process are fodder.

ON THE OTHER HAND...

Are they not just harmless, delightful evenings full of nice frocks and jewels and peacocking and clapping and praise and fun?

Why SHOULDN'T we publicly celebrate the outstanding folk in our line of business?

I know!

I'm totally conflicted.

Mostly, I find it all cringeworthy and indulgent beyond belief. Vainglorious.

So, I made a decision, quietly (not now obviously!), to absent myself from such events, even if nominated.

This has been, on the whole, the right decision for me. I find it easier not to participate. That way, I don't have to fight with my own inner conflicts about it.

In reality, what do I do? I watch it all play out on the telly, peeking from behind my fingers and occasionally shouting threats of incalculable violence at certain individuals or certain decisions. This assuages my irritation and feelings of injustice.

Better, of course, would be to check out entirely, ignore it all, and not be drawn in. I know that, but I'm a hopeless, helpless and consummate nosey parker, and I simply can't resist.

How twatty is that?!

CHOOSE A LANE, FRENCH.

So, over the years, various award offers have surfaced and I've managed to navigate my way around them with very little fuss. In the end, it seems it's perfectly easy to give the award to whoever's on the list instead, in most circumstances. I'm not sure what that says for the voting systems.

I guess they're adaptable.

And this is right, actually.

You can't, and shouldn't, have it both ways. Either turn up and receive it or stay away and go without. And shut up.

Whilst I've been getting vertigo, so very high is my horse, Ms Fatty Saunders has no such dilemma. She has the rather healthy attitude that it's all a preposterous game and that it needs to be dealt with lightly and taken with a fistful of salt.

If she's nominated, she goes, she often wins and she accepts with grace. I see the efficacy of this approach.

I wish I could authentically do the same, rather than sitting on the sidelines grumbling about it all under my breath, like Muttley from *Wacky Races*.

So, there we have it. Seems straightforward, don't it?

Except, of course, I'm in a double act.

So, sometimes the award is for us both, and I think that my stance has, on occasion, denied Fatty the chance to win. That bit is not OK. Luckily, she is a mensch and has never made it difficult for me.

Until . . . 2009, when we, The French AND The Saunders, were offered the Bafta Fellowship.

Which is quite bigknobs.

I was in the habit of side-stepping, so it was form for me to say a speedy but polite nay. She seemed to accept this and I didn't think twice about it.

Until.

We went out for dinner one evening with our other halves. There was a reference made to this fellowship award.

Me – Meh.

I went to the loo.

As I came out of the bathroom, Jennifer was there, waiting.

She blocked my exit.

This was serious. She spoke frankly. Suffice to say we'd had a few drinks, so she was fuelled and, let's say, persuasive.

Fatty – Listen, I don't want this to be a thing but, seriously, I'd like us to accept this award. It's a huge honour, it's not in competition with anyone else, the last double act to receive it was Morecambe and Wise, my mother would be so delighted, as would all the family, as would yours... come on...

Me – Well... umm...

Fatty – Plus, the BAFTA building is right next to Piccadilly Circus. It's so central. We'd have a lifetime membership. They have toilets.

We're getting older.

Think about it . . .

Free toilets in Central London?

Me – OK, deal.

And that was that. We received the BAFTA Fellowship.

It's a lil' thing called COMPROMISE mixed with a lil' thing called LOVE mixed with a lil' thing called INCONTINENCE.

#1
TWAT

A CALL TO ARMS

(And legs. And heads. And hearts.
And bosoms. And fannies. And willies.)

I can't emphasize enough the positive impact I've felt on writing down these stories to share with you. I had a sneaking feeling I would really enjoy writing this book, but I had no idea of its effect on me, and if you can feel even a tiny bit of that too, then that will be bleddy marvellous.

Truthfully, the point of it all at the outset was very simple: I wanted to have some fun. I know that some of the most wonderful memories of my life thus far have been the joys of sharing how I feel in those most arse-wrenching moments of cringe with my friends and family. Some of the incidents are such that you can ONLY share them with your closest beloveds, because those are the ones most likely to understand and, in some cases, forgive your foolishness without judging you (much). They are also likely to be the folk who know you well enough to appreciate and relish your story alongside you, anticipating how you might be feeling or how you might react. It's almost doubly delightful for them. They are your safe space to unzip. So to speak. They are the folk who will hold you while you unleash all your embarrassment, all your humiliation, all your mess.

What I DID NOT know, until now, is that this doesn't just apply to my most beloveds. It seems, miraculously, that you, my readers, ARE also beloveds, because I utterly, honestly know and trust my bones that you will receive these stories in the spirit I offer them.

And THAT, my dearios . . .

Has been a revelation.

What it implies is huge.

It means that, without doubt, it is a basic human need to share stories of our idiocy just as much as stories of our successes, our trials and our wonder.

Only when we offer up our softer underbelly of culpable silliness can we truly connect with the same in others. In other words, when I trust you to receive a story with love and laughs wrapped around it, I implicitly promise to do the same with yours. I invite you to tell me those stories, which may even be the places you have quietly, secretly been hiding your embarrassments?

It's a massively liberating experience to openly admit and tell.

Tell with gusto.

Tell with confidence.

Tell with cheek.

Polish up your story for effect and savour the embellishments because you are doing that for the pleasure of others, and for the sheer joy of the joke that is a mistake, or a misjudgement.

Sorry (not sorry) to sound all gooey about it, but I've come to the conclusion that in the telling and in the receiving of stories like this, there are indisputable acts of love.

I know.

Hear me out.

Sometimes, the mistakes we make, the faux pas, the blunders, the insensitivities, are the home of shame. They stick to us like painful burrs, difficult to shake off and always hurting.

I am learning not to allow mistakes to inhibit me or haunt me.

I'm stepping INTO them, hosting them with acceptance, embracing them. I refuse to let all my mistakes define me as a sum of their parts alone.

Of course, I surely AM that idiot who made those errors but, more importantly, I am also the one who wrangled them into tales I retold myself and others for fun, and I'm the one who learnt from them.

I hope.

That is THE WHOLE POINT of blunders.

To learn,

To feel their sting,

To move on from.

Success and achievements don't teach you half as much as mistakes.

It's in the nip of the failure that my most keen, tinglingly clear understanding takes place.

To wrangle the big power of a mistake into a small funny thing to suit your future purposes is honestly utterly marvellous.

It means you are more in charge.

You can chase away the shame that accompanies your flaws.

It's like a darkness.

If you shine a light on it, it vanishes. You can flush out the embarrassment by owning it and brightening it up.

That, for me, is HUGE.

It means that by telling my could-easily-be-shameful stories, I am lighter.

By listening to others' stories, they are lighter.
Tons of affirmation and approval are gifted therein. So easily.

And it feels completely LOVELY.

The honesty and fun connect us.

The twat in me sees the twat in you.

And loves it. A lot.

We can so effortlessly lift the lid off any of each other's hurts, simply by joining in.

That's the key.

JOIN IN.

Don't let shame hamper you, don't conceal your mistakes. Instead, wear them like badges across your ample (or otherwise) chesticles, for all to see.

I promise, it will make you feel more authentic and it will help others relate to you.

Because it's truthful. Simple as.

Mistakes make you memorable.

Mistakes tell us about ourselves.

Mistakes tell us about others.

Mistakes are hilarious.

Mistakes expose our flaws.

Mistakes show us ourselves honestly.

Mistakes are mirrors.

Mistakes are gloriously human.

There's such a grace in accepting our flawed selves. And there's such relief!

How come it's taken me sixty-five years to know this?!

And ...

Whilst I'm indulgently gobbing off like this, might I also make a heartfelt plea to return to something that seems to have gone completely out of fashion ...?

Which is . . .

The straightforward power of the GENUINE APOLOGY?

Which, of course, goes hand-in-hand with most slip-ups in life.

Or ought to, at least.

I've noticed that more and more, we've descended into the realms of the fake apology.

Y'know –

The ones that start with . . .

'I'm sorry you took it that way.'

'I'm sorry but . . .'

'I'm sorry if . . .'

'I'm sorry you hate me.'

'I don't know how many sorrys you want.'

'I'm sorry, but you know me . . .'

'I'm sorry, if you are.'

'I'm sorry I was telling you a difficult truth.'

'I'm sorry for all the bad stuff I've ever done.'

'Sorry, fine, sorry, OK?'

Those kinds of bollox.

Those aren't apologies, they don't fix anything. We are ALL always going to make mistakes. Some of those mistakes might affect others. All that is needed, in my experience, to rebuild a valued relationship is to be real.

Just own it and mean it.

SAY:

'I'm sorry. I'm truly sorry. I was a twat.'

Simple. The twat word encapsulates it all.

That mends it in most cases, believe me.

And that, in itself, is another ACT OF LOVE.

I only pass this on as a suggestion because I'm an old bird and I have learnt it the hard way.

Yet, as so often is the case, the right way is so bleedin' obvious.

Our impact on others is huge.

I've also learnt this. Finally.

People will sometimes quote something we did together, or something I've casually said, which has stuck with them long after I've forgotten it.

I've had the same with others – and I can't believe that they have forgotten some seminal (for me) moment.

So – try to remember that someone has a laugh when they remember such and such a moment involving you . . .

Clangers and fails feature massively in this department, so don't undervalue them.

Share them.

It's significant.

You are significant.

You are thought about.

You are remembered.

Often via your mistakes.

I read a lovely thing recently, and I'm sorry I can't remember exactly where, but it was about how gemstones get their bright colour from their 'impurities' or 'structural defects'.

YEP.

True of humans also, I reckon.

It's time, folks, to step up and into our fullest twatness and celebrate everything about it.

Let's accept and enjoy the fact that we are ALL pretty much 90 per cent knob.

I'm a TWAT and, frankly, it's not negotiable.

Deal with it.

We don't do perfect here.

TWATS RULE!

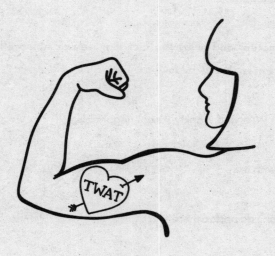

PS A COUPLE OF TINY EXTRA RECENT TWATLETS

FOOD

It probably isn't that surprising to learn that I think about food quite a lot. I realized recently that I'm always planning my next meal, very often when I'm eating my current meal. I love a bit of order in life and I like to plan the food. That way, I can sort of eat it with my imagination as well as actually eat it when it finally turns up. Double yum.

You know that game where you choose what your final meal might be if you were, say, going to be executed? Well, I play that game with myself pretty much ALL the time. I operate as if each meal is my last, so as to savour every morsel. Before you say it or think it – yes, I'm aware what this food fantasizing looks like when it comes to eating disorders and all-round slightly bonkers of mind-ness – but I honestly don't give a poo.

It's my hobby.

And it's such a pleasure.

Those who know me well will have witnessed me weeping softly on occasion, as I lift a particularly tasty pasty to my lips. Because the thought of it being my last is so very sad, it spirals me into a despondent void.

YES, I KNOW I'VE INVENTED THE FANTASY!

THANK YOU FOR POINTING IT OUT.

LET ME JUST 'ENJOY' IT FOR A MINUTE, PLEASE!

I have even found myself imagining that certain favourite foodstuffs might be about to become extinct.

(On reflection, this is clearly me kidding myself in order to eat more in the moment.)

I know ...

But I've had some heart-stoppingly panicked moments convincing myself that I might never see peas again.

Or scampi.

Or katsu sauce.

Or Wotsits. Especially giant Wotsits.

Oh, the sorrow.

On the other hand, I'm no guru, I have no clever secrets to the ways of happiness. All I know is that I've never felt dejected with a Curly Wurly in my hand, and that's an indisputable factoid.

On the rare occasions in my life where I've followed strict diets for whatever reason, I have been totally scuppered by particular incidents, like when I decided to give up bread, which I managed for over a year of hellish torture. I simultaneously decided to give up cheese, another of my true loves.

I lost quite a lot of weight since these were two of my biggest sins.

Then.

Then.

Then . . .

Lucifer at my local deli decided to combine them, and he made cheesy bread. No one on earth should be expected to resist that.

I accepted the devil into my life and have, ever since, imagined that each tasty cheesy bread loaf is, indeed, the last that will EVER be baked.

What a twat.

'OTHERS'

We recently moved house and I am getting used to our new gaff and all its noises and smells. It's an old house, so there are plenty of both.

I stole the master bedroom, which has the best view, and I've converted it into my office, where I'm writing these very words right now. It's bright pink and I love it.

I placed my desk at the window so that I can see the lovely Tamar River. So, most of the room is BEHIND me.

A couple of weeks ago, I heard some strange tapping behind my back.

I dismissed it at first.

But it persisted.

Each day, tap tap tap.

Nothing and nobody else was in the room.

The cat is always asleep on the window ledge.

The dog is curled up at my feet.

The tapping is from elsewhere.

Of course, I let my worst tortured imaginings run wild.

I see — we have surely bought a house built on an ancient tribal American Indian gravesite (in Cornwall). Our home is a certain portal to all the unresting souls who will no doubt scream their yawling, undead pain into my ears for years to come. I will become possessed and demented as they inhabit me on their tormented journey through the open wound of their purgatory.

I am to be a vessel of horror.

The tapping is just the start.

Tap. Tap. Tap.

I decided to do the only right thing, and when I next heard it, I physically addressed my ghostly housemates, out loud. I stood up and faced into the room:

Me – I know you're here. I have moved into this house. I mean you no harm. I hope we can live alongside each other in peace. Please DO NOT show yourself to me. No offence, but I really don't want to see you. I will have to leave this place if you do. Maybe that's what you want, I don't know. But listen, if I go, someone else will come along and probably will call in an exorcist or something and it won't go well for you guys … so … y'know, let's live in paranormal harmony side by side, just like in the award-winning and very well-written TV show *Ghosts*, which is both funny and heart-warming. Let's do it like that, OK? In the meantime, um … peace be with you … and … um … yes … AMEN … and … I love you.

I sat back at my desk and tried to work.

Tap. Tap. Tap.

A sure sign they'd heard me, I thought. An affirmation of sorts.

Two days later, my husband was working from home in the daytime. I'd told him about our spirit friends and how it was freaking me out a bit.

He brought me a cuppa and while he stood near me, the phantasms had the nerve to start it up again …

Tap. Tap. Tap.

I shushed him.

Me – Listen, that's it! That's what I've been telling you about! They're communicating with me . . .

Husband – That's the noise?

Me – Yes!

Husband – Dawn, that's the central heating. The pipes run right under those boards in the middle of this room. Don't you remember . . . ?

Umm...

Right, OK, no ghosts then.

Just some pipes and hot water.

I spoke aloud to those pipes.

That's me, folks, a certified pillock of the community.

CHOCOLATE FOUNTAIN

OK, this is my last story for now, OK?

Many moons ago, we recorded an episode of *Vicar of Dibley* where I stuck my head into a giant chocolate fountain – and then the Archbishop of Canterbury turned up. We pre-recorded this scene because it was going to be messy. We shot it as the last scene of the day.

I was covered in sticky chocolate.

It had been a total hoot.

It was the evening by the time we finished.

I went back to my dressing room (this was at Shepperton, so the dressing rooms are some distance from the studio and mine was at the end of a long corridor). The wardrobe department told me to leave my messy chocolate-soaked clothes in a heap they would collect in the morning.

I stripped off, I climbed into the shower, it was bliss. It had been a long ol' day and the warm water was a merciful salve to my tired flesh and bones.

The melted chocolate was stubborn and stuck to my hair. It took six shampoos to get it out, but finally I did.

I dried myself and my matted hair and I climbed into my own clothes to go home at last.

It was late.

I gathered up my bag, my coat, turned off the lights around the mirror and headed to the door.

Somehow, somehow, somehow, I don't know how – my door was jammed shut with a broken lock.

It would NOT open.

I was three floors up.

Everyone had gone home.

EVERYONE.

I didn't own a mobile phone back then . . .

So, I just had to shout . . . the resounding echo of a total and epic twat.

HELLOOOO!

HELLOOOO!

I'M STUCK IN HERE!

HELLLLLLLLLOOOOOOOOOOOOOOOO

ACKNOWLEDGEMENTS

To Lovely Sue, with all my twatty heart

To all my twatty team at Penguin

especially Lou, Jill and Liz

To all my darlin' family, Ma Biggs, Biggs, Billie, Lils

and Olly and the FANTASTIC Esme

To the home guard – Sammy, Dave, Janet, Tim,

Laura, Dave E, Mike B and Kelvin

To the BFF and the Gusband

To Goodie and Mowzer for the company

And finally . . . To the giantly-talented twat that is

Jessika Green, for all the fab doodles

Also by Dawn French

Because of You

Me. You. A Diary

According to Yes

Oh Dear Silvia

A Tiny Bit Marvellous

Dear Fatty